MAHAN

KW-222-670

Poland

Berlitz Publishing Company, Inc.

Princeton   Mexico City   London   Eschborn   Singapore

Berlitz Trademark Reg. U.S. Patent Office and other countries
Marca Registrada

Text:	Neil Schlecht
Editor:	Media Content Marketing, Inc.
Photography:	Neil Schlecht
Cover Photo:	Neil Schlecht
Layout:	Media Content Marketing, Inc.
Cartography:	Raffaele De Gennaro

Although the publisher tries to insure the accuracy of all the information in this book, changes are inevitable and errors may result. The publisher cannot be responsible for any resulting loss, inconvenience, or injury. If you find an error in this guide, please let the editors know by writing to Berlitz Publishing Company, 400 Alexander Park, Princeton, NJ 08540-6306.

ISBN 2-8315-7886-8

Printed in Italy
010/201 NEW

CONTENTS

● A (☞ in the text denotes a highly recommended sight

Poland

POLAND AND THE POLISH PEOPLE

Even though the country is more than 1,000 years old, Poland's survival is a bit of a miracle. Its boundaries were continually redrawn over the course of eight centuries. And then suddenly the nation fell off the map. For 123 years Poland, wedged in the middle of Europe, ceased to exist for the world's cartographers.

Partitioned for a third time at the end of the 18th century by Prussia, Austria and Russia, Poland—ground zero in the battle between East and West—was reduced to a promise and a prayer for Poles, and the object of tug-of-war for more powerful states.

But that was only the beginning of Poland's troubles. Then the real tragedy occurred. Hitler and the Nazis invaded Poland, launching World War II, then extinguished many of its cities and eradicated 20 percent of its people, including nearly its entire Jewish population of three-and-a-half million—until then the largest Jewish community in Europe. Wars have befallen many countries in modern times, but few have been as thoroughly ravaged as Poland.

Yet Poland rebuilt itself from the smoking rubble of war. From photographs, paintings, architectural drawings, and the memories of its grief-stricken survivors, Poles reconstructed the Old Towns of Warsaw and Gdańsk brick by brick—only to suffer four decades of imposed Communist rule and grudging submission behind the Iron Curtain. Poland again rebounded. Labor strife in the 1980s was one of the sparks that triggered the demise of Communism throughout the Soviet bloc. Poland, remarkably, is today poised to enter the European Union as a modern and independent nation.

Syrena, the legendary mermaid of Warsaw, wields her sword and shield in the city's Market Square.

It is one of the world's great modern recovery stories. Poland has survived with its culture, language, spirit, and most of its territory intact.

Largely rural, Poland has great tracts of wilderness and primeval forest in its 22 National Parks. But the country is perhaps best known for ancient towns rich with history and architecture. Kraków, which survived unscathed from the war, is a splendid medieval city with a magnificent market square, castle complex on a hill, and one of Europe's oldest and most prestigious universities. Its beauty is on a par with Prague or Budapest, and the city, the royal capital for 500 years, is surprisingly vibrant, young, and modern.

Warsaw, Poland's largest city by far and its commercial and political capital, is not the bleak gray morass of Communist days. True, it can be chaotic, unrefined and unaesthetic, but it perhaps best expresses Poland's current crossroads. A 20-minute walk can take you from the Royal Castle to a monolith of Stalinist architecture to the gleaming headquarters of international companies banking on Poland's emergence as a major European player.

While Warsaw's Old Town is an astonishing phoenix-like fable of reconstruction, Gdańsk's historic center is even more alluring, its Royal Way a loving restoration that defies the imagination. No matter how many times you stroll through the medieval layouts of these cities over cobblestoned streets, gazing at stunning examples of Gothic, Renaissance, and Baroque architecture created in—can it be?—1953, you cannot help but be flabbergasted. The buildings look old and feel ancient. It is as though the indefatigable Polish people willed their authenticity.

Smaller towns are nearly as impressive. Zamość is a perfect Renaissance town with one of the most photogenic main squares in the country. Zakopane is an Alpine town carved out of wood at the foot of the High Tatra, the highest peaks of the Carpathian Mountains, in easy range of great hiking and skiing. Toruń, the home of the great astronomer Nicholas Copernicus, is a red-brick feast of Gothic architecture, while Poznań, a determined trade center, puts the market into its extraordinary Old Market Square.

Poland is a nation of 39 million, the size of Spain. Its people are fervently Catholic—more than 80 percent call themselves practicing Catholics—and more conservative than many of their Western European neighbors. Throughout most of its history, Poland was an intensely cosmopolitan place, with Germans, Jews, Lithuanians, Belarussians, Armenians, and others living within its borders. During the Second Republic (1919–1939), only

In the heart of Kraków's Old Town, the world's largest medieval market square.

In some old Polish towns, such as alpine Zakopane, you might feel as if you've arrived in another era.

two-thirds of the people were ethnic Poles. It has also traditionally been a land of religious tolerance. When medieval Europe was rocked by religious wars, Poland was a safe haven for Jewish, Protestant, and Orthodox refugees — making the intolerance later inflicted by Germany on Polish territory all the more terrible.

Today, Poland is unusually homogenous: 98 percent of the people are Poles. The Jewish population was reduced to 250,000 after the Second World War, and today there are no more than a few thousand Jews living in Poland. The largest groups of minorities are Lithuanians, Ukrainians, and Belorussians.

Literacy rates are high, at 98 percent. Poles are well-educated, and young people in the larger cities speak English (much more so than German or Russian) with the same fluidity and enthusiasm of those a couple of border lines west. They're just as up-to-date on fashions, trends and music; they have cell phones glued to their ears and e-mail accounts they tap into daily at Internet cafés across the country.

Of course, the vast Polish countryside is a much different story. Here you'll still see a stubbornly traditional way of life that seems years, if not decades, slower than city life. Little-trafficked roads are lined with wooden shrines, erected by plain folk intent on manifesting their devotion. Even if you're not planning on traveling through the countryside, you can get a good taste of rural life by visiting a skansen, or outdoor ethnographic museum, which makes the ways of Polish country life accessible by relocating historic houses and civic buildings from small villages to open-air exhibitions.

Poland's history as a territory coveted by great powers all around it ensured that the north-south divisions often seen elsewhere are, here, primarily east-west divisions. The west is more Germanic, organized, pragmatic, and industrious, while the East has a reputation of being more Russian—which means, in short, relaxed, cultural, and introspective. Poznań, for example, halfway between Berlin and Warsaw, revels in its business skills and organizational attitude. Kraków, the ancient capital much closer to Ukraine than Germany, is just as proud of its free-flowing cultural prowess and its status as a place where art and education override business (except, of course, for the business of tourism).

The asymmetrical towers of St. Mary's church in Kraków, one of Poland's most distinctive landmarks.

There has always been a cultural struggle between East and West in Poland. The Poles are a Slavic people, like their Ukrainian, Russian, and Lithuanian neighbors to the east. Yet their historical and cultural connections to the West are formidable. The Catholic Poles first took their religious cues from the West in the 10th century, and cultural epochs basic to Western Europe—the Enlightenment and the Renaissance— were just as much a part of Polish society. The shared identity, as well as the uneasy conflicts, between East and West have defined this land in ways that go far beyond geography.

Although Poland has suffered a checkered political and military past, it has been the source of glorious achievements in the arts and sciences. Poland claims such greats as the 19th-century composer Frédéric Chopin, the novelist Joseph Conrad, Madame Curie (the Nobel Prize winner in chemistry and physics), and the Nobel Prize winners in literature Henryk Sienkiewicz, Władysław Reymont, Wislawa Szymborska, and Czesław Miłosz.

Life post-Communism has had, predictably, its growing pains. Though by most any measure Poland, along with Hungary and the Czech Republic, has made incredible strides in a scant 12 years after the break-up of the Soviet Union, many of its citizens and international institutions feel that the transition to privatization and democracy hasn't been as smooth or as rapid as they'd hoped. Immediately after gaining political and economic freedom in 1989, Poland found itself without state support, and production plummeted. While there was a huge spurt in growth and prosperity in the mid-1990s, unemployment has recently increased dramatically. The gap between Western and Central Europe still hasn't closed. Gross domestic product is less than a quarter of that in EU countries. Beyond questions of privatization and growth, Poland and the other countries hoping for admittance to the EU must establish a viable legal system capable of ensuring economic safeguards.

Poles are eager to embark on the road to European integration and full development of a stable free-market economy with benefits across society. Yet Poles are not likely to race ahead without remembering the past and the often-fractured road that has brought them to this point. They are intensely proud that Copernicus, who "stopped the sun and moved the Earth" and revolutionized the way we understood our universe, was a Pole. They revel in the fact that Poland

Poznań stands on land settled by the Polonian tribe, people responsible for the foundations of the Polish language.

signed the second-oldest Constitution, delineating government powers, after the United States. Poles young and old live with the horrors of death-camp atrocities committed on their soil. They turn out in great adoring hordes for native son Pope John Paul II, known to them as Karol Wojtyła, former Archbishop of Kraków. And the Polish people recognize the role that a little-known shipyard electrician in Gdańsk had, first as a leader of the Solidarity union and then as Poland's first elected president since 1922, in indelibly changing the events of the second half of the 20th century.

Poland may only now be developing as a destination for many of the world's travelers. But it is certainly no stranger to the world stage.

A BRIEF HISTORY OF POLAND

Poland's war-torn and almost incomprehensibly fractured history plays out like an epic novel—occasionally triumphant, frequently sad and tragic. Over a millennium, Poland evolved from a huge and imposing, economically powerful kingdom to a partitioned nation that ceased to exist on world maps for over 120 years, and finally to a people and land at the center of the 20th century's greatest wars and most horrific human tragedies. But Poland has survived, with its culture, language and most of its territory intact, and today Poles look forward with optimism to taking their place at the forefront of the new, post-Communist Central Europe.

Foundations of the Polish State

The region that would become Poland, a great plain sandwiched between the Vistula and Odra rivers, has been inhabited since the Stone Age by migratory tribal peoples— among them Celts, Balts, Huns, Slavs and Mongols. Tribal culture reigned, untouched by the more sophisticated civilization of the Roman Empire. Slavic tribes arrived by the eighth century A.D. and put down roots; the Ślężanie, Mazowszanie, Pomorzanie and Wiślanie peoples inhabited much of the territory. The Polonian tribe, which settled the area that today is western Poland around Poznań, provided the foundations for the development of a Polish language and nation.

Prince Mieszko, leader of the Piast dynasty that ruled the Polonians, undertook the bold step to unify the Polanie (literally, "people of the fields") and neighboring tribes. Mieszko adopted Christianity—most likely a savvy political

Old Town Square in Poznań, one of Poland's oldest settlements and today one of its most dynamic cities.

move to place the new state on equal footing with nearby Christian states with ties to Rome—and married a Czech princess, Dobrava, in 965. His religious conversion won him the support of the papacy, and Mieszko effectively founded the Polish state the following year. By the end of the 10th century, he had united his tribal territory, Wielkopolska (Great Poland), with that of another tribe, Małopolska (Little Poland)—regional names that remain current today. Silesia, settled by a different tribe, would eventually become the third component of the nascent Polish state.

Mieszko's son Bolesław "The Brave" was crowned by Otto III, the Holy Roman Emperor. Bolesław later repelled invasions from Otto's successor and then sought Poland's own expansion eastward; he eventually annexed parts of present-day Ukraine. The Pope recognized Bolesław as the first king of Poland in 1025, elevating the country to full membership in a European community of Christian states.

Duke Bolesław Krzywousty divided the country into four provinces to be ruled by his sons. Kraków grew in importance and eventually became the country's capital in the 12th century (replacing Gniezno), when Duke Bolesław "the Wry Mouthed" established his official residence on Wawel Hill. Kraków was better positioned for trade and also less vulnerable to attacks from the Czechs and Germans. Helped by the arrival of immigrants from all over Europe, including thousands of Jews, Kraków became a prosperous and culturally enriched capital.

Beginning in the mid-13th century, Tartars invaded Poland on three occasions. Threatened by the Prussians, Duke Konrad of Mazovia invited the Order of the Teutonic Knights in to help defend against them. The Knights used their considerable military might to then assume control of the very territory they had helped defend, capturing Gdańsk, securing most of the Baltic region and cutting off the rest of Poland from access to the sea. The Tartars defeated the Poles at the Battle of Legnica and destroyed most of Kraków, leaving only the castle and St. Andrew's Church intact.

Kazimierz the Great & the Jagiellonians

The last king of the Piast dynasty, Kazimierz the Great, succeeded in reunifying

Ancient fortifications still stand in Kraków, Poland's original 12th-century capital.

Poland. His rule ushered in Poland's first golden age. Kazimierz built great castles and towns, codified laws, and created an entire administrative system of governance for the war-torn country. He rebuilt Kraków with magnificent architecture and established the country's first university there. Kazimierz, a pragmatist, did not try to wrest control of Silesia, in the hands of Bohemia, or the territory seized by the independent state of the Teutonic Knights. Instead, he consolidated the state by expanding eastward and accepting minority populations, including persecuted Jews from across Europe, into the predominantly Catholic nation.

Kazimierz's death in 1370 left the crown to his nephew, Louis of Anjou, the King of Hungary. One of his daughters, Jadwiga, succeeded Louis in Poland, while the other assumed control of Hungary. Jadwiga's 1386 marriage to Jagiełło, the Grand Duke of Lithuania, led to Poland's strategic alliance with that powerful country. After his wife's death, Jagiełło ruled both Poland and Lithuania for nearly half a century, establishing a dynasty that would remain in power until 1572. The united countries defeated the Teutonic Knights at the Battle of Grunwald in 1410 and repelled Germanic eastward expansion. The Thirteen Years' War yielded great benefits for Poland: the transformation of Danzig (formerly Gdańsk) into an independent city-state under the protection of the Polish crown and the capture of other Knights territories.

Polish nobles saw their political might expanded during the beginning of the Renaissance with the king's "rule of the nobility," which granted exclusive right to enact legislation to nobles in the parliament of Sejm. The 1500s were a time of prosperity, power, and cultural and scientific achievement for the Polish-Lithuanian Commonwealth. In 1543 Nicholas Copernicus, born in Toruń and a graduate of the Jagiellonian University in Kraków, published his groundbreaking and astronomy-altering treatise, *De revolutionibus orbium Coeliestium,* which positioned the sun and not the earth as the center of the universe. Although the Reformation and Lutherism had an impact on Poland, the country largely avoided the devastating religious wars that raged elsewhere in Europe.

The Sejm moved to Warsaw in 1569, and the death of the last ruler of the Jagiellonian dynasty, Zygmunt August, led to the creation of a Republic of Nobles and an elective monarchy that would serve it. Warsaw, more strategically located in the center of the country, became the official capital of Poland in 1596. King Sigismund Vasa moved the royal residence from Kraków's Wawel Hill to Warsaw in 1609.

The Swedes Are Coming

Three successive elected kings emerged from the Waza dynasty of Sweden. Sweden had become the strongest military power in Europe after the Thirty Years' War, and in the mid-17th century, it set its expansionist sights on Poland. The Swedes invaded Poland in 1648, an event labeled the "Swedish Deluge" in Polish history books. The devastating war lasted five years, during which time Sweden was able to capture most of Poland. The war and the disastrous effects of the plague decimated the population of Poland, reducing it to just four million, roughly half its total in the early 17th century.

Remarkably, Poland retained enough military might to repel the Ottoman Turks in their advance through the Balkans. The military leader Jan Sobieski defeated Turkish troops at the Battle of Chocim in 1673, and Sobieski would later be credited with saving Vienna from Turkish forces (and thwarting the Ottoman Empire's designs on Western Europe). Sobieski was elected king of Poland, but his attentions to battles against the Turks at the expense of domestic affairs did not bode well for him and Poland.

Decline and Partitioning

At the beginning of the 18th century, Poland entered a prolonged period of decline, marked by financial ruin, a debilitated military, and a series of ineffectual kings. Poland was transformed into a client state of the Russians, and then lost much of its western territory to the Prussians during the Silesian Wars that ended in 1763. The following year Stanisław August Poniatowski was elected the last king of the Polish-Lithuanian Commonwealth, and Poland soon faced one of its most humiliating episodes.

The powerful Prussians came up with a plan to partition Poland, which gained the support of the Russians. The imposed treaty in 1772 robbed Poland of nearly a third of its lands. Yet Poniatowski recovered to preside over a reform movement that precipitated the creation of the 1791 Constitution, which restored the hereditary monarchy and overhauled Poland's political system. The liberal constitution, the oldest in the modern world after that of the United States, provided for the separation of powers among legislative, judicial and executive branches of the government.

In Toruń the Copernicus Museum pays tribute to one of Poland's and the world's most influential scientists.

Kraków's St. Mary's Church has already been destroyed and rebuilt twice during the city's tumultuous history.

None of these reforms pleased the Russians and Prussians, who continued to covet Polish territory. Russia invaded Poland and in 1792-1793 it, along with Prussia, imposed a second partition of Poland, annulling the constitution and essentially divying up the country between them. Tadeusz Kościuszko, a hero of the American War of Independence, led a military insurrection in 1794, defeating the Russians with a mostly peasant army. The uprising was quashed, however, and in 1795, Poniatowski was forced to abdicate. A third partition crushed Poland and placed the country under the control of Austria, Prussia, and Russia. Poland ceased to exist—its very name was abolished by treaty—for the next 123 years. Warsaw went to Prussia, Kraków to Austria.

In desperation, Poland looked to Napoleon Bonaparte and Revolutionary France for assistance against its oppressors. Napoleon defeated the Prussian army in several key battles and established a semi-independent Duchy of Warsaw from 1807 to 1815. Napoleon gained an ally in Józef Poniatowski, a heralded military leader and the nephew of the last king. The 1812 Polish War re-established the Poland-Lithuania border, but

Napoleon's troops were crushed as they advanced on Moscow. Napoleon suffered a great defeat, but his ally Poniatowski refused to surrender, preferring to sacrifice himself and his troops. The suicidal mission became an important rallying cry for Poles during the remainder of the 19th century.

The Congress of Vienna of 1815, with an aim to reorganize Europe after Napoleon's escapades, did not re-establish an independent Poland. Rather, it again partitioned the country, placing the territory of the Duchy of Warsaw under the control of the Russian czar. For three decades, Kraków existed as an independent city-state, though it was again incorporated into the Austrian partition in 1846.

The former Duchy of Warsaw, called the Congress Kingdom, enjoyed some autonomy and prosperity in the early 19th century. Poles launched a series of armed insurrections against its occupiers in 1830 and, after defeat, again in 1846 and 1863. The last rebellion counted on support from England and France that never arrived. Many Poles, fearful that an independent Poland would never again be realized, emigrated to France and then the United States during this period. Those who remained focused on preserving Polish language and culture if not the Polish state.

The Aftermath of World War I

The next pivotal episode in Polish history coincided with the end of World War I and the defeat of the Russians, Germans, and Austrians. The partition of Poland collapsed in 1918, and Poland's bid for independence won the support of American president Woodrow Wilson and the Bolshevik government in Russia. The Polish war hero Józef Piłsudski, released from a German prison, took control of Poland. Yet just two years later, the Soviets invaded and surrounded Warsaw. Piłsudski and his troops managed to hold back the Soviets.

In 1926, Piłsudski engineered a military coup and seized control under the Sanacja, or senate, government that would rule until the start of World War II. By 1933, Poland was sandwiched between two dictatorships: Stalin in Russia on the eastern border, and Hitler in Nazi Germany to the west. Both fixed their eyes on occupying Poland, and they signed the ruthless Nazi-Soviet Pact in 1939, which stated that either would be free to pursue expansionist acts without the interference of the other. In the agreement was a secret clause providing for the eventual full partition of Poland between Germany and Russia—even though Poland had signed 10-year non-aggression pacts with both.

Nazi Invasion, World War II & the Holocaust

In September 1939, the Nazis invaded Poland. The annexation of Danzig (Gdańsk) marked the official start of World War II. Soon after, German forces launched an occupation of Kraków, where they based their governing body, and laid siege to Warsaw. The Soviets invaded Poland less than 10 days later, following the terms of the pact signed with Germany.

The Nazis initiated a ruthless campaign in 1940, rounding up intellectuals, Jews, and others, executing some in the streets and deporting others to concentration camps in the occupied territory. The Germans constructed walled Jewish ghettoes in Warsaw and Kraków. At death camps like Auschwitz and Birkenau, near Kraków, the Nazis eventually murdered millions of Poles, as well as other prisoners from across Europe. The Soviets themselves imprisoned some 1.5 million Poles in labor camps of their own and eliminated potential "troublemakers" through actions like the Katyn massacre, in which 4,500 Polish military officers were summarily executed.

From 1941 to 1944, all of Poland fell under Nazi occupation, and the country became the focus of Hitler's campaign to exterminate all Jews and non-Aryans. Hitler invaded the Soviet Union in 1941, an act that drew the Soviets and Poles together in a shaky alliance.

A heroic uprising in 1943, led by poorly armed Jews in the Warsaw ghetto, lasted a month until Nazi reinforcements annihilated it and reported back to Germany that "Warsaw's Jewish quarter has ceased to exist." The following year, Poland's Home Army initiated a surprise attack against the occupying Nazis in Warsaw, and awaited assistance from the Soviet Red Army, perched on the outskirts of the capital. The military support never came, and as his troops fled the city after quashing the insurgency, Hitler ordered them to raze Warsaw building-by-building and thereby annihilate important monuments of Polish culture. When the Soviets entered the city, they found it reduced to rubble and ashes.

The second World War was more devastating for Poland than any other country. Six million Poles lost their lives dur-

Warsaw's Old Town, along with the rest of the city, has had an incredible resurrection since being razed by Hitler's forces.

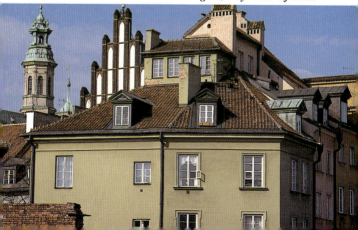

ing World War II, and the Jewish population was decimated, reduced from 3 million to just a couple thousand. Poland lost a significant amount of territory after new borders were drawn up in the Yalta Agreement in 1945, including the eastern regions around Wilno (Vilnius) and Lwów (Lvov). The Polish borders shifted west a couple of hundred kilometers, incorporating ancient parts of Silesia like Wrocław that had belonged to Germany before the war. Poland also regained Danzig, which had not been a part of Poland since its seizure by the Teutonic Knights.

Communism & Soviet Domination

In the aftermath of the war, Poland was Sovietized, with the installation of a Soviet-friendly communist regime, the nationalization of businesses, confiscation of church property, and forced exile of political and religious leaders. With Soviet aid, a rebuilding program was initiated, an

effort that reconstructed the Old Towns of Warsaw and Gdańsk, among others, in costly and meticulous efforts based on paintings, photographs and architectural drawings. The Soviet Union signaled its domination over Poland with the 1955 "gift" of the Palace of Culture and Science in

The grim entrance to Auschwitz, Poland's notorious Nazi concentration camp.

Warsaw, a monstrous skyscraper that would become a hated symbol of foreign influence.

Many Poles, especially among the intellectual and professional classes, opposed Soviet influence and Communist rule, and in 1956 the regime faced its first real test. Worker strikes and protests erupted in Poznań, and spread into armed confrontations in the streets. Security forces opened fire on rioters and killed some 80 people. A weakened and suddenly unstable Communist Party installed former First Secretary Gomulka as leader without consulting Moscow, an event that prompted Soviet, East German, and Czech troops to amass on the Polish borders. A similar uprising occurred in Hungary the same year, and the Soviets invaded to quickly crush it.

But the episode in Poland, called Polish October, exposed fissures in the Communist regime, and it served as the impetus for a slight relaxation of censorship, religious repression, and economic controls. Reforms stalled, however, and the following decade saw a return to strict Soviet doctrine. The 1970s were marked by inflation and the emphatic snuffing of strikes and protests. Living standards dropped dramatically, and the Soviet Union was forced to prop up the Polish economy.

Pope John Paul II & Solidarity

In 1978, the Polish Cardinal and Archbishop of Kraków Karol Wojtyła was elected Pope; he took the name John Paul II. A staunch opponent of the Communist regime, Wojtyła returned to Poland in 1979 as Pope and drew great, thunderous crowds at every stop. The following year, unrest grew among workers after 100% increases in food prices. Lech Wałęsa, a shipyard electrician, led worker strikes in Gdańsk. The size and vehemence of their protests, which spread countrywide, forced the government to negotiate with the Solidarność (Solidarity) trade union, granting its workers' demands and allowing free

Birkenau (also called Auschwitz II) was constructed by Hitler to further his extermination "solution" for the Jews.

trade unions limited autonomy to oversee their industries. Viewed from hindsight, Solidarity was critical in establishing the foundations for opposition to Communist rule across Central and Eastern Europe.

General Wojciech Jaruzelski adopted a hard line and declared martial law in December 1981 in response to continued strikes across Poland. He initiated a military takeover of the Communist Party, and the government arrested thousands of Solidarity activists and sympathizers, banned the trade union, and suspended civil rights. Two years later, the regime lifted martial law after the Pope's second visit to Poland, and Lech Wałęsa won the Nobel Peace Prize in 1983, familiarizing the world with the struggles of Polish workers. The government's resolve did not abate, however. In 1984, the Polish secret police murdered Father Jerzy Popiełuszko, an outspoken supporter of Solidarność. The Warsaw priest had been set to be beatified by the Catholic Church—on his way to becoming a saint.

The mid-1980s witnessed a gradual program of liberalization in Poland on the heels of Mikhail Gorbachev's remarkable perestroika and glasnost in the Soviet Union, the promises of greater openness and economic freedoms. The economic crisis in Poland persisted, though, and mass strikes were staged, even as Gorbachev visited Poland. In 1989, talks established the basis for limited power-sharing between the Communist Party and Solidarity.

The End of Communist Rule

Desperate austerity measures failed to jump-start the economy. In semi-free elections, Solidarity was the overwhelming victor, and the Communist regime collapsed. On 9 December 1990, Poles made Lech Wałęsa the first popularly elected president in post-World War II Poland, a watershed event for the Soviet bloc of nations. In 1991, Wałęsa met with the Pope in the Vatican and the Warsaw Pact was dissolved.

Poland's road to capitalism and democracy has been a complicated one. Wałęsa fell out of favor with Poles and was defeated in the 1995 elections. But by that time, the country had joined the World Trade organization, and the European Union had agreed to open negotiations to admit Poland (along with the Czech Republic, Hungary, Slovakia, and Slovenia) into the EU.

By the end of the 20th century, Poland had joined NATO, and a decision on EU membership was expected by 2003. Poland is thought by most experts to be among the few countries that will be allowed to join in the first round of decisions. In June 1999, Pope John Paul II visited his homeland for the eighth time as Pope, and he was again received by enormous crowds, proof once again that Poland's committed Catholics and fervent patriots had survived the Communist years with their faith and pride intact.

WHERE TO GO

Poland, bordering the Baltic Sea to the north, Germany to the west, the Czech Republic and Slovakia to the south, and other former members of the Soviet Union (Ukraine, Belarus, Lithuania, and Russia) to the east, is large and predominantly rural. The main points of interest for first-time visitors are the principal cities, beginning with Kraków, Warsaw and Gdańsk — whose old towns certainly rank among the finest of Central Europe, or Europe, for that matter — and smaller, well-preserved towns that are rich in history, architecture, and Polish character. It is also a place to see great castles, memorials of Jewish culture that trace unspeakable tragedy, and churches and synagogues that are sites of important Catholic and Jewish pilgrimage.

It's easy and inexpensive to get around Poland by train, probably the preferred method of navigating the country. Exploring the Polish countryside, which seems several decades, if not more, behind the cities, requires either a lot of time and patience, or an automobile. And even one's personal transport can be slow-going, as the Polish road system lags behind its speedy development in other areas. For visitors with plenty of time, the mountains, sea, and lake districts have much to offer, but this guide deals primarily with the major Polish cities and towns.

Because Kraków is such an overwhelming draw for most visitors, this section begins there, in southeast Poland. Just beyond Kraków, reached in easy day trips, are the fantastic 700-year-old Wieliczka salt mine and the horrendous physical legacy of Nazi concentration camps in Auschwitz and Birkenau. In southern Poland, along the Slovakian border, are the Tatra Mountains and the delightful ski resort town of Zakopane. To the southeast, between

Kraków's Market Square in the heart of Old Town buzzes as a hub of activity for people of all ages.

Kraków and Ukraine, is the 16th-century Renaissance town Zamość. Almost in the exact geographical center of Poland is the present-day capital and commercial center, Warsaw. In north and northwest Poland are Gdańsk (formerly Danzig) on the Baltic, and nearby Malbork Castle, the most splendid fortification in Poland. Toruń was the birthplace of the great Polish astronomer Copernicus, while Poznań is one of the most ancient centers in Poland and today one of its most dynamic cities.

> **Kraków is said to have more than 125 churches — with 60 of them in the Old Town alone.**

Café relaxation in Cloth Hall — once a headquarters for cloth merchants, its sellers now target tourists.

KRAKÓW

Elegant Kraków, the ancient royal capital of Poland, is one of the finest old cities in Europe. More than a thousand years old, and the country's capital for half that time, Kraków is the third-largest city with 750,000 people. It is also considered the heart and soul of Poland, home to many of its greatest artists, writers, musicians, filmmakers, and one of the world's oldest universities. It

> When Kraków was occupied by the Nazis, the Main Market Square was renamed "Adolf Hitler Platz."

is one of the few major towns in Poland not devastated by the World Wars of the 20th century, and its miraculously preserved medieval market square and castle hill make it Poland's most seductive city.

Though awe-inspiring churches, monuments, and museums line its ancient streets, and the historic royal castle overlooks the old town from a hilltop, Kraków is one of Poland's liveliest and hippest cities. It abounds with young, fashionable café-hoppers. Kraków's roster of taverns and cafés, many of them idiosyncratic places in underground cellars, are among the city's undeniable highlights. Most everything of interest in Kraków is easily managed on foot (most of the streets in the Old Town are pedestrian-only), with the possible exception of Kazimierz, the old Jewish quarter that lies just a few kilometers south of Old Town. Though a visitor could rush through Kraków and "see" its Old Town and Wawel Hill in a couple of days, one would miss out on much of the alluring character of the city, which is best savored over several days or a week.

Main Market Square & Old Town

Kraków's layout dates to 1257 and remains unchanged to this day. The charming streets are lined with historic townhouses, fine churches, and delightful small shops. The whole of Old Town (Stare Miasto) is encircled by the moat-like **Planty**, a ring of relaxing parklands where massive fortifications (and indeed, a wide moat) once protected the city. The best place to begin to get to know Kraków is Europe's largest medieval **Market Square** (Rynek Główny), at the heart of the Old Town. The spectacular square pulsates with youthful energy at all hours, and its sidewalk cafés are fine places to enjoy the views of the square and the parade of Kraków's most fashionable denizens (and flight of the huge flock of pigeons). Many of the houses that line the square have Neo-Classical façades, though they are considerably older than that, and are full of interesting architectural details.

At the center of the square is the **Cloth Hall** (Sukiennice Hall), built in the 14th century and reconstructed after a fire in 1555 in the Renaissance style (the arcades were added in the 19th century). The building once housed the richest of Kraków's cloth merchants, and today its first-floor stalls are occupied by privileged sellers of amber jewelry, religious artifacts, art, and souvenirs targeting Kraków's year-round tourist trade. Indeed, the entire market square was once overrun with merchants of all kinds, though today the only ones permitted are flower sellers (as well as booths set up for special fairs). Upstairs is the **Cloth Hall Gallery**, a small but impressive museum of Polish painters from the 18th to 20th centuries, including the paintings of the royal court of Poland's last king, Stanisław Poniatowski. The museum, part of the National Museum and one of Kraków's earliest (1879) galleries, holds the work of one of Poland's greatest painters, Jan Matejko, whose huge canvasses exclaim the glories of Polish history. One of Matejko's most famous works, at the far end of the room dedicated to his art, is "Homage of Prussia," dealing with the 1525 Teutonic pledge of loyalty to the Polish king. Look also for "The Death of Elenai" by Jacek Malczewski, Józef Chełmoński's "Master of Horses," and "Ecstasy," a controversial late-19th-century painting of woman and beast by Wladyslaw Podkowinski.

Next to Cloth Hall are the remnants of the 15th-century **Town Hall Tower**, the rest of which came down in the early 19th century. Southeast of it is tiny **St. Adalbert's Church** (Kościół Św. Wojciecha). Intriguingly, the copper-domed 11th-century church is a couple of steps below the level of the square. The **History Museum of Kraków**, at Rynek Główny no. 35 in the former Krzysztofory Palace, contains a large collection of documents, paintings and model buildings attesting to the development of the city.

On the eastern side of the square, just beyond a statue of the renowned poet Adam Mickiewicz and allegorical figures — a hangout for local youths and backpackers from around the globe — is **St. Mary's Church** (Kościół Mariacki). The asymmetrical towers and turret-surrounded spire are one of Kraków's most celebrated images. A church from 1220 first stood on this spot, and it faced east, as was the custom of the day. St. Mary's, built on the original foundations in the 14th century, also sits at an angle to the square.

The main entrance to St. Mary's, a Baroque porch façade, is used only by those attending Mass. Tourists are asked to enter through the side door, along the passageway (St. Mary's Square) off Rynek Główny. Inside is a stunning burst of ornamentation and color, with extraordinary wall paintings by Jan Matejko in blue, green, and pink. The ceiling of the main nave is painted a bold blue with

The Trumpeter

Every hour, a trumpeter appears in the high tower of St. Mary's to play the Hejnał Mariacki, a call to arms that began as a warning of the advancing Tartar army in 1241. The tradition has been practiced uninterrupted for several centuries. The bugle call ends mid-bar, a symbol of the story that the lone watchman was felled by an arrow as he warned the city. Watch the trumpeter from the passageway just south of the church; at the end of the piece, he waves to those gathered below.

gold stars. The highlight, though, is the sumptuous altar-piece, a masterwork of Polish Gothic that took the 15th-century German artist Veit Stoss a dozen years to create, beneath five tall columns of stained-glass windows. The powerful altarpiece depicts the Dormition of the Virgin Mary, flanked by scenes of the life of Christ and the Virgin. Over the central nave is a massive crucifix; at the rear of the church is Art Nouveau stained glass, the work of Kraków's Stanisław Wyspiański, behind the organ loft.

The courtyard next to St. Mary's leads to **St. Barbara's Church** and a passageway onto **Little Market Square** (Mały Rynek), where colorful façades adorn what was once the site of meat, fish, and poultry vendors (whose wares were moved from the Main Market Square owing to their unpleasant odors).

One of the main streets leading off the Main Market Square is ul. Floriańska, a busy pedestrian-only street full of shops, restaurants, and cafés. At no. 41 is the **Jan Matejko House**, the home where the 19th-century Polish master was born, worked, and died. It includes memorabilia and a number of paintings from his personal collection, and much of the house stands as the artist left it upon his death in 1893. At the end of the street, and the edge of Old Town, is the **Floriańska Gate**, one of the original seven gates in the city's fortified walls. Built in 1300, it is the only one to have survived 19th-century modernization plans. An outdoor art market is set up here daily, and pictures executed in every conceivable style blanket the stone walls. The view down Floriańska toward the spire of St. Mary's is one of the most priceless in Kraków.

Flower sellers brighten the Market Square, with a background of cloudy sky and St. Mary's Church.

Just beyond the gate is the **Barbican**, a circular brick bastion built at the end of the 15th century and one of the few remaining structures of the medieval fortifications. It was originally connected to the Floriańska Gate over the moat. On nearby ul. Szpitalna are two buildings of significance. One is the **Church of the Holy Cross**, a small 15th-century church with splendid Gothic vaulting, and the other is the eclectic **Słowacki Theater** (on Pl. Św. Ducha 1), a bright yellow-and-green-roofed structure built in 1893 and modeled after the Paris Opera House. Don't miss the curious laughing gargoyles on the rooftop.

At the top of ul. Św. Jana, the street running parallel and just to the west of Floriańska, is one of the highlights of Old Town, the **Czartoryski Museum**. This splendid museum in an immaculate palace contains a coveted portrait by Leonardo da Vinci ("Lady with an Ermine"), one of just three known oil portraits attributed to the great master and considered a worthy rival to Mona Lisa. The stunning small painting, of a slender young woman with a bony hand stroking a curious little animal, was repeatedly ferreted in and out of Poland to elude would-be thieves. In fact, the empty frame across the room from La Dame à l'Hermine is that of a Rafael portrait that didn't fare as well: It was stolen by the Nazis and never recovered. The museum also houses a great collection of Polish silver, early ecclesiastical relics from France, handsome groups of medieval religious art and military instruments, and an intriguing Rembrandt landscape, flush with minute detail and metaphorical meaning. Beyond the

> Bracka street, famous for its artists' studios, is also unique because it is one of just two in the Old Town grid that is not straight, indicating that it predates the 13th-century origins of the rest of the city.

art works gathered is the intrinsic interest of visiting a palace belonging to one of Kraków's most prominent families, who were collectors on a grand scale.

Fans of early religious art will want to stop in the **Szołajski House**, at (Szczepański Square 9). This branch of the National Museum, in a 17th-century house, holds a huge collection of Gothic and early Renaissance works, including altarpieces from area churches and a famous *Madonna* from Kruzlowa that dates to 1400.

The area south and west of the main market square is home to the famed **Jagiellonian University**, the oldest university in Poland and one of the oldest in Europe, and several fine churches. Take any of the streets heading west from the square, such as Św. Anny. Enter a small door

Gargoyles cackle atop the green-roofed Słowacki Theater, modeled after the Paris Opera House.

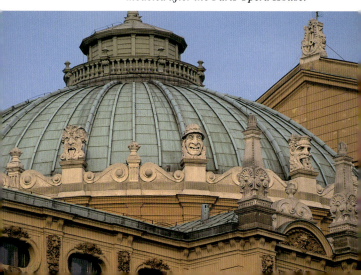

Kraków is home to the extraordinary Gothic architecture of the Collegium Maius.

beneath the Flemish-style roof to the **Collegium Maius** (ul. Jagiellońska 15), the main building of the university and a beautiful 15th-century Gothic structure with an arcaded central courtyard and marble fountain. Be sure to note the fanciful drainage pipe heads, of medieval dragons and the like, on the rooftop. King Kazimierz founded the university in 1364, but its golden age dates to the period of the reign of King Jagiełło, for whom it is named. Copernicus studied here in the 16th century, and the guided visit inside to the University Museum — including several ornate academic halls, the treasury, library, and professors' dining hall — shows off several objects related to the university's most famous collegian and his theory that revolutionized our notion of the universe, including astronomical instruments, a registrar's book signed "Mikołaj Kopernik," and a very rare globe, dating back to 1520, with the earliest known depiction of the Americas. Visits are conducted primarily in English, though the gentleman who generally leads the tours is conversant in several European languages. Pope John Paul II received an honorary doctorate at the university, where Latin is still compulsory, and Poland's most recent Nobel Prize winner for literature donated her medal and a good portion of the prize to the museum.

The streets near here are always flush with students — Kraków has nearly 100,000 university students attending 12 universities and academic institutes. Around the corner from the Collegium Maius on Św. Anny is the **Church of St. Anne**, linked to the university and a favorite of marrying students. The 17th-century interior is a superb example of airy Polish baroque, with a high dome, spectacular stucco work and wall murals. Facing the Planty is the **Collegium Novum**, a late 19th-century Neo-Gothic building decorated with the crests of the university and its most celebrated benefactors. When Hitler's troops invaded Kraków in 1939, they stormed this hall and arrested nearly 200 professors and academicians, and hauled them off to concentration camps.

On ul. Franciszkańska, directly south of the market square, is the **Franciscan Church and Monastery**, dating from 1269. The gutted interior was rebuilt in the 19th century after the last of four disastrous fires. Relatively unassuming from the exterior, the exuberant interior is a stunning assembly of brilliant stained glass and colorful wall paintings in floral and geomet-

The Renaissance-style Sigismund Chapel sparkles among Wawel Cathedral's many architectural gems.

ric motifs. At the rear above the organ loft is a remarkable Art Nouveau stained-glass window designed by the local artist Stanisław Wyspiański, a disciple of Jan Matejko, in 1900. The large "Act of Creation" depicts God the Father in wild streaks of color. Wyspiański reportedly based God's face on the countenance of a beggar, his mother's brother. The stained-glass windows behind the altar, also by Wyspiański, depict the Blessed Salomea to the left and St. Francis to the right. To the right of the altar is a passage to the Gothic cloisters, worth a look for its 15th-century frescoes and portraits of the bishops of Kraków. The painting at the end of the hall is of the "lady who stopped the fire," a reference to the great fire of 1850 that was miraculously snuffed out at that very wall of the Franciscan church.

Due east, the street changes names to reflect the presence of another religious order and its 13th-century church, the **Dominican Church and Monastery** (ul. Dominikańska at Stolarska). It too suffered greatly from fire damage, and today is notable principally for its Neo-Gothic chapels and original 15th-century portal. The monastery has serene Gothic cloisters.

Heading east toward Wawel hill, along ul. Grodzka, is the **Basilica of SS Peter and Paul**, recognized by a large dome and long row of stately statues of the Twelve Apostles out front. The oldest Baroque building in Kraków, the basilica was founded by the Jesuits in the early 1600s. The rather austere late-Renaissance interior has recently been renovated.

The small Romanesque church next door is **St. Andrew's**, dating from the 11th century and thus one of the oldest churches in Kraków. Its colorful history includes a stint as a hiding place and fortress for Poles battling invading Tartars in 1241.

Across the square facing those two churches, turn down cobblestoned ul. Kanonicza, one of Kraków's most charming streets. Along the way to Wawel hill, at no. 9, is the **Wyspiański Museum**, where

Stanisław Wyspiański completed a series of drawings for 48 stained-glass windows, depicting the whole of Polish history, he hoped would someday replace those in the Wawel cathedral. There are now plans to execute the windows, but for technical reasons, they will not be installed in the cathedral as was Wyspiański's dream.

the famous Kraków artist lived and worked in the early 20th century. Wyspiański is perhaps best known for his stained glass and decorative frescoes (as seen in the Franciscan Church), but he was also a poet, designer, and dramatist. On view are many of his paintings, drawings, theater set pieces, and sketches for his dramatic stained-glass windows, including the set of 48 he dreamed of installing in Wawel Cathedral, part of a comprehensive plan to transform the royal palace into a complex called the Acropolis.

Just down the street, at no. 19, is the **Archdiocesan Museum**, where Pope John Paul II lived on two occasions, first as a young priest and then as Bishop of Kraków. The quarters, houses dating from the 14th century, are now home to a small museum of interesting 13th - 20th century religious art, including a collection of Gothic sculptures of the Madonna and child, and artifacts belonging to the Pope, including the room where he lived (with his desk, bed and two pairs of skis), photographs, and ornate gifts from heads of state and religious leaders.

Wawel Hill

A castle or royal palace has existed on Wawel Hill overlooking the old town of Kraków since the ninth century, though the area may have been inhabited as early as the Paleolithic Age. The first kings of Poland maintained a royal residence here from the 10th century until King Sigismund Vasa moved the royal seat to Warsaw in 1609. Over the centuries it was repeatedly destroyed by invaders and war, ultimately transformed into the complex that today is a mix of Gothic, Renaissance, Baroque, and Neo-Classical architecture. Wawel, a symbol of the Polish

About Tickets to Wawel

Separate tickets are needed for the cathedral and castle complexes. Guided group visits are available at the main box office past the cathedral (there are two other box offices, including one on the path on the way up the hill). The component parts of Wawel have different opening hours, so be sure to check the hours in "Selected Hours & Admissions." The Royal Chambers, Treasury and Armoury, and Lost Wawel are free on Sundays.

nation, is a great source of national pride to Poles, and it is a popular place of spiritual pilgrimage. Principally visited are the royal castle and chambers, treasury and armory, the cathedral and royal tombs, and Sigismund stairs to the bell-tower. The best way to reach Wawel is to hike the lane up the hill at the end of ul. Kanonicza. Expect crowds and large tour groups, especially in summer, and allow at least three hours for a full visit.

The Gothic edifice of **Wawel Cathedral** — what one sees today is the third cathedral built on this site — was begun in 1320, some three centuries after the first. The site of half a millennium of royal coronations and burials, it is

Kraków's Franciscan Church contains a stunning array of stained glass, in addition to wondrous wall paintings.

the final resting place of nearly all the Polish kings. The entrance is marked by a curious set of mammoth bones—a rhinoceros—that were found on the premises and are said to protect the cathedral and all Kraków against those who would attempt to harm the city.

At the center of the nave is an ornate **shrine to St. Stanislaus**, the 13th-century bishop of Kraków who was martyred by the Polish king Bolesław in 1079. The saint's body was partitioned and, according to legend, it re-formed and became whole again — a sign taken as a portent that a divided Poland, partitioned by Germany, Russia, and Austria, would also reconstitute itself. The cathedral witnessed the coronation of 32 kings, each of whom knelt before the shrine and asked St. Stanislaus for forgiveness. Of particular interest among the various tombs, altars, and chapels is the extraordinarily ornamented, Renaissance-style **Sigismund Chapel** designed by the Italian architect Bartolomeo Berrecci (it's the one with the gleaming golden dome seen from outside). To the right of the entrance, the **Holy Cross Chapel** is a feast of extraordinary 14th-century Byzantine frescoes and a late-15th century marble sarcophagus. The chapel, the burial chamber of King Jagiełło, was being meticulously restored in 2001.

The tight, wooden 14th-century stairs leading to the **Sigismund Belltower** are not for the claustrophobic or lame, but for the athletically inclined they're a fun climb up to see the revered Zygmunt bell, which dates to the mid-16th century and is the largest bell in Poland, requiring eight people to ring it. Krakovians say they can hear the bell from as far as 20 km (12 miles) away when it is rung on major holidays.

Behind the altar is the tomb of Kazimierz the Great, the so-called "Builder of Poland." The mausoleums of the

Sigismund kings, beloved Queen Jadwiga and others lie upstairs in the cathedral, while downstairs in the **Royal Crypts** are the tombs of 10 Polish kings and their families, as well as a handful of national military and literary heroes. The entrance to the tombs is toward the back of the church, and the exit is onto the main castle courtyard.

In the **Treasury** is a repository of religious and royal objects, including illuminated texts, even though the Prussians

The Sigismund Chapel of the Wawel Cathedral is named for one of Poland's greatest kings.

stole the entire stock of crowns at the end of the 18th century and had them melted down.

Wawel Castle, also an enduring symbol of Polish nationhood, was the royal residence until 1609, when it was moved to Warsaw. King Bolesław built the first and considerably smaller residence in the 11th century, but it became a grand, Gothic palace during the reign of Kazimierz the Great in the 14th century. A great fire razed it in 1499, and the elegant Renaissance palace that was rebuilt by King Zygmunt is largely the structure one sees today. Swedes, Prussians, and Austrians all overran and occupied the castle and its grounds, and the last group of invaders destroyed churches and built military barracks, leaving the hill with an oddly empty square and large and rather unappealing buildings to the west of the castle. The Polish government and people did not recover Wawel until the end of World War I in 1918, when the partition of Poland ended.

Jews in the war-time ghetto were required by the Nazis to: have a Star of David designating all businesses; carry Jewish identity cards at all times; and ride on the back half of trams, which were labeled "Fur Juden" (for Jews). (See page 53.)

Visits are restricted to five sections of the castle. Purchase tickets in the passageway between the cathedral and castle.

The **Royal Chambers** are the largest and most interesting part of the castle. They have been nicely restored to their original Renaissance style and furnished with Baroque and Renaissance furniture, much of which is not original but certainly representative of royal lifestyle. The most impressive and valuable items on display are without doubt the spectacular collection of 16th-century Flemish tapestries commissioned by King Sigismund. Only 136 of the original 364

Figures carved from salt in the Wieliczka Salt Mine, an extraordinary subterranean destination.

pieces (all ordered at the same time) survive, and not all are on view. The tapestries have a peripatetic history. At various times, many were stolen and others taken out of the country for safekeeping. After World War II, they traveled from Romania to France and England and finally Canada before being recovered for Poland in 1968.

Also on view is a handsome collection of 17th-century Turkish tents in an exhibition of Oriental Art.

The **Deputies Hall**, or Throne Room, is also called the "Heads Room," a name that becomes obvious once you glance at the ceiling. It is festooned with small carved wooden heads of some 30 citizens of Renaissance Kraków — normal folks, not just royalty, nobles and clergy as might be expected. Over the king's throne is a stunning Flemish tapestry. The **Senators' Room** is wall-to-wall with tapestries placed over the windows, reportedly so there would be no outside distractions during important Senate sessions. It is the only room where the exact placement of tapestries is known.

The **Treasury & Armoury**, in vaulted Gothic rooms that were part of the 14th-century castle, house the royal collection of weaponry and spoils of war, including a Royal Jagged Sword present at all Polish coronations from the early 14th century on. An exhibit called **Lost Wawel**, south of the cathedral, is an interesting display of remnants of Wawel from the 10th century, including archaeological finds and the foundations of the first church in Kraków, the Romanesque Rotunda of SS Felix and Adauctus, which was destroyed by the Austrians. Enter Lost Wawel from outside the castle (take a left out of the courtyard). As if that's not enough, at the foot of the hill, Wawel also has a **Dragon's Cave**, according to legend the home of a reclusive dragon, the Smok Wawelski. After descending into the cave, you emerge on the banks of the Vistula River.

KAZIMIERZ

Kazimierz, home to the ancient Jewish quarter that became a war-zone Jewish ghetto during the Nazi occupation of Kraków, was built in 1335 as an independent, planned, and walled town by the Polish king whose name it took. Jews, persecuted throughout Europe, were offered refuge in Kraków. However, King Jan Olbracht moved Kraków's entire Jewish population to Kazimierz at the end of the 15th century. Today the district is essentially a suburb within easy walking distance or a short tram ride from the Old Town of Kraków.

Before the war, some 60,000 Jews lived in the Kraków area. Only a few thousand remained in 1945, and today there are reportedly as few as 200 here. After decades of neglect, having been robbed of its people and soul if not all its buildings after the war, Kazimierz is undergoing a revitalization. Jewish foundations from around the world are funding the restoration of historic buildings, and Steven Spielberg brought new attention to the quarter with his Academy Award-winning 1994 film *Schindler's List*, much of which was filmed in the area. As visitors to Kraków discover Kazimierz, new hotels, cafés, and restaurants are moving in, and there are

> Fans of Steven Spielberg's film *Schindler's List* will recognize many of its locations in Kazimierz and Podgórze. The Jewish bookstore Jarden (ul. Szeroka 2; tel. 429.1374) arranges "Schindler sightseeing tours" of the district. The attention the movie brought to Polish Jews might counterbalance the questionable notion of Holocaust-related tourism.

signs that young Krakovians now see it for more than the devastating reminder of a shameful period in Polish history. Some Jews are even beginning to return and attempt to claim stolen property.

The easiest way to get to Kazimierz is to take the blue express tram no. 3 south from the Planty just outside Old Town and get off at the third stop along Starowiślna. If walking from Wawel Hill, take Stradomska, which becomes Krakoska, south and turn left at Józefa.

Among dilapidated buildings and new businesses in the Jewish quarter are many signs and insignias of the Jewish population. Eight synagogues (of the 30 that once existed here) survived the war, but only one still functions today as a house of worship. A couple of others have been established as museums. Ul. Szeroka, which means "large street" but is actually more of a square, was the heart of the district in the 15th century. On the west side of the square is the **Remu'h Synagogue and Cemetery**, a small 500-year-old synagogue that remains active. The second-oldest in the district, it is perhaps the most important synagogue in the area today. Jews visit to touch the chair of the 16th-century Rabbi Moses Isserles, a great philosopher and lawyer, and a black feast calendar is one of the few surviving elements of the original synagogue. Much of the cemetery next door was destroyed by the Nazis, though several hundred gravestones, many of them 400 years old and buried by the Jews themselves to avoid desecration by invaders of the 18th century, were discovered during excavations after the war. The handful of tombs enclosed by a fence includes that of Rabbi Isserles, which is often covered with small stones, measures of respect left behind by Jewish visitors. Legend holds that the Nazis were in the process of leveling the rabbi's grave along with all the others when one of the workers was felled by a heart attack. The Wailing Wall at one end of the cemetery is made up of fragments of gravestones that were destroyed by the Germans.

At the south end of Szeroka is the **Old Synagogue** (Stara Synagoga). Dating to the 15th century, it is the oldest surviving Jewish building in Poland. Today it houses a museum of Jewish history and culture, with an ornate original 16th-century wrought-iron bimah, or pulpit, in the center of the main prayer hall. Upstairs is an exhibit of Nazi newspapers and photographs depicting the hateful ghettoization of Kazimierz.

One block west is the large **Isaac Synagogue** (Synagoga Isaaka, at ul. Kupa 18), a cavernous hall that was once the most beautiful of all the synagogues here, with opulent Baroque stucco decoration from the mid-17th century that was destroyed by the Nazis. Today school groups and other visitors sit silently and watch a somber documentary of Jewish life ("The Memory of Polish Jews") set to wailing music that evokes the Holocaust on televisions at the end of the otherwise empty room. Next to the synagogue is an atmospheric, bohemian café, **Singer**. Diffuse light wafts past red velvet curtains of the darkened tavern, where most of the tables are old Singer sewing machines.

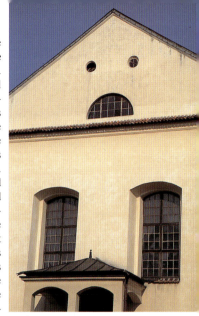

The Isaac Synagogue, once the most opulent synagogue in Kraków, is now little more than a cavernous hall.

The **Jewish Cultural Center** is located just west of Pl. Nowy, the main Jewish marketplace, on ul. Meiselsa. It has regular exhibits and conferences aimed at preserving knowledge of Jewish culture.

Western Kazimierz is the Catholic section of the planned town and is marked by three churches: **Corpus Christi** Church (along Józefa street), Gothic St. Catherine (ul. Skałeczna) and the **Pauline Church and Monastery**. Celebrated cultural figures, including Stanisław Wyspiański, are buried in the crypt of the last, where it is also said that Kraków's St. Adalbert was mutilated and then miraculously resurrected. On Pl. Wolnica is the old town hall, which now houses an **Ethnographic Museum**, said to be the largest in the country, with exhibits of rural Poland and folk traditions.

The **New Cemetery** (on ul. Miodowa 55, a short walk

northeast of Szeroka, across the railroad tracks) is a large, haunted place of toppled tombstones with Yiddish insignias and lettering grown over by bright green moss. The "new" Jewish cemetery was founded in 1800 and, though appearing wholly abandoned today, is the only current burial place for Jews in Kraków.

The actual ghetto where the Nazis forced the Jews to live between 1941 and 1943 is located across the river and Powstancóv bridge at the end of ul. Starowiślna, in the Podgórze district. Here you'll find another place of

The New Cemetery, founded in 1800, remains today the only burial place for Jews in Kraków.

interest and pilgrimage, the **Pharmacy Under the Eagles** (Apteka pod Orłem, on Pl. Bhaterów Getta 18). Now a small museum of Jewish life in the ghetto, it was once a pharmacy belonging to a Pole — the only non-Jew whom the Germans allowed to live in the ghetto — who witnessed the murders of 1000 Jews in the square, Ulmschlag Platz, across the street and decided to give shelter to as many Jews as he could. Tadeusz Pankiewicz later was one of the critical witnesses at the Nuremberg trials. Nearby, off ul. Lwowska to the southwest of the pharmacy, is a still-standing section of the wall that the Nazis constructed around the ghetto. If the top of the wall looks familiar, it is because Hitler's agents designed the wall to mimic the form of traditional Jewish tombstones, the message delivered a clear "here is where you shall die." Oskar Schindler's old Emalia enamel factory still stands at the edge of Podgórze, on ul. Lipowa, though today it has been recast as an electronics factory.

Most visitors to Kraków limit themselves to the Old Town and Wawel Hill, and perhaps the Kazimierz Jewish Quarter and side trips to **Auschwitz concentration camp** and **Wieliczka Salt Mine** (see page 54). If you have more time in the city, though, just outside Old Town is the **National Museum** (Muzeum Narodowe), on Al. 3 Maja 1 (the museum is a block north of ul. Pułaskiego, heading west from Old Town). The rather off-putting, Soviet-style architecture and poorly illuminated, forgotten feel of the place slowly give way to an important collection of 14th-century stained glass and decorative arts, furniture, and vestments from Wawel palace, and a wide array of military armaments and uniforms, which will be of greatest interest to history buffs. It also hosts most important itinerary exhibitions that come to Kraków.

For something completely different, and of special interest to architecture and Japanese culture buffs, visit the **Manggha Center of Japanese Art & Technology**, across the river south of Wawel Hill and west of Kazimierz (ul. Konopnickiej 26). The splendid futuristic building, by the Japanese architect Arata Isozaki, holds a collection of Samurai armor, pottery, and woodblock prints. The museum was initiated by one of Poland's most famous film directors, Andrzej Wajda, who won the Kyoto prize and donated the earnings to establish the center.

EXCURSIONS FROM KRAKÓW

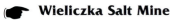 ## Wieliczka Salt Mine

Wieliczka (pronounced "vee-uhl-eechka"), a salt mine more than 700 years old located about 15 km (9 miles) southeast of Kraków, makes for an extraordinary subterranean adventure. The mine reaches 327 m (1073 ft) and nine levels underground. Visitors descend 378 steps down to the first level of 64 m (210 ft) and then pass through two miles of tunnels, visiting some 20 chambers and chapels carved out of salt by miners. The St. Anthony Chapel dates to 1698. But the largest and most astounding chapel is the **Chapel of the Blessed St. Kinga**. Everything in it is carved out of salt. Its chandeliers, altar, and remarkable relief carving (with great perspective) of the Last Supper were created over a period of 70 years, beginning in the 19th century, by just three miners, who were obviously talented and dedicated sculptors (like all the chapels and chambers, this massive hall was carved in the miners' off-hours). Weddings are occasionally held in the St. Kinga Chapel, as is Mass three times a year. Along the way in other chambers you'll also see green-salt statues of Copernicus and even, curiously, the Seven Dwarves.

Protected by UNESCO as a World Heritage monument, the mine was the property of the Polish Royal Family (for whom the salt, called "gray gold," contributed one-third of the total royal wealth) until the 1772 partition of Poland, when it fell to the Austrians. The mine was first visited by Copernicus in the 15th century. Salt mining continued here until 1996, and today the mine is visited by tour groups and those seeking relief from respiratory ailments like asthma in the sanatorium 200 m (656 ft) below the ground. During World War II, the Nazis used the tallest chamber (which measures 36 m/118 ft to the ceiling) as a secret factory for airplane parts, staffed by Jewish prisoners. A few years back, a couple of crazies pulled off a bungee jump and others conducted the first underground balloon flight, documented by the Guinness Book of World Records, in the same chamber.

During July and August, a miners' orchestra plays in the lake chamber, treating visitors to a 170-year-old tradition.

At the end of the two-hour visit to the mine, you can either visit the museum of mining equipment and geological specimens (separate ticket required) or be whisked back to ground level by a rickety wooden elevator.

Visitors to Wieliczka must be accompanied by guides.

Add a little flavor to the décor — the chandeliers at Wieliczka are a salty touch.

Individuals can join established groups in either Polish or English (if there is none in English, you could purchase an English-language guide and tag along behind a Polish group, without missing much). To get to Wieliczka, the cheapest and most efficient means is to take a "contra-bus" marked "Wieliczka-Kraków" at the train station in Kraków (cost per person, 2 zł). To book guides in advance, a good idea in summer when groups can overrun the mine, call Tel. 278.7302).

Auschwitz & Birkenau

Poland was ground zero for Nazi Germany's reprehensible campaign to rid the world of all Jews, and the Auschwitz and Birkenau concentration camps were two of the most efficient cogs in their killing machine. Visiting them is a chilling and unforgettable experience.

The International Festival of Highland Culture is held every August in Zakopane. Essentially a week-long mountain folklore contest and full schedule of concerts, music competitions, and parades, it has been held since 1968, and is an excellent introduction to the unique mountain culture of the Góral people. (See page 60.)

At Birkenau, an inscription bluntly reads: "Forever let this place be a cry of despair and a warning to Humanity, where the Nazis murdered about one and a half million men, women, and children, mainly Jews from various countries of Europe." The horrors of the acts that were carried out here, and the reality of lost lives and potential, is unfathomable.

Auschwitz (Oświęcim being the name of the Polish town where the camp is located) was originally a Polish army barracks about 60 km (45 miles) west of Kraków. Jews from as far away as Norway and Greece were loaded

Brace yourself before a visit to the Birkenau concentration camp. A disturbing experience awaits you.

into wretched, sealed trains with no water, food, or bathrooms, and very little air to breathe, and herded to the concentration camps in Poland. The first Polish "prisoners of war" were brought here in June 1940. After that, streams of Jews, as well as Soviet prisoners, were relocated to the camps. They became slave laborers; many died of starvation, while some were summarily executed and many others were herded into gas chambers and killed with lethal Zyklon B (cyanide) gas.

Poland

A short and disturbing documentary film is shown in English, German and French at regular intervals. Its original footage, shot by the Soviet troops who liberated the camp in 1945, is a good, if startling, introduction for trying to comprehend what you're about to see. After viewing the film, pass under the famous gates of entry to Auschwitz, which cruelly read "Arbeit Macht Frei" (Work Makes Free). About 30 cell blocks, as well as watchtowers and barbed-wire fences, survived the Nazi attempt to destroy the camp when they fled at the conclusion of the war. You can walk freely among the blocks and enter those that are open. In one,

The guard tower and fences at Auschwitz, a jarring reminder of the atrocities humans are capable of committing.

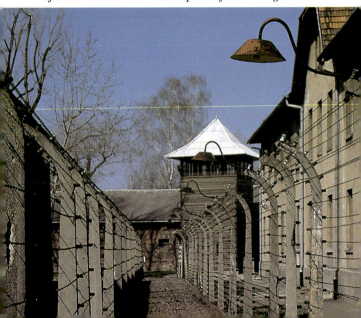

behind glass cases you'll see collections of piles of shoes, twisted eyeglasses, tons of human hair, and suitcases with the names and addresses of prisoners — who were told they were simply being relocated to a new town — stenciled on them. Hallways are lined with row upon row of mug shots of the prisoners, some adorned with flowers from surviving family members. Outside Block 11, the so-called "Block of Death," is an execution wall where prisoners were shot to death. Inside is where the Nazis carried out their first experiments gassing prisoners with Zyklon B. Another barrack nearby is dedicated to the "Martyrdom of the Jewish People." At the end of the exhibit of historical documents and photographs, a haunting and mournful soundtrack, the song "Oh God the Merciful," plays while the names of people killed at death camps are read.

Birkenau (also called Auschwitz II), about 3 km (2 miles) from Auschwitz, was built in 1941 when Hitler went beyond simply collecting political prisoners and embarked on a mass extermination program. Its 300 long barracks on 175 hectares (523 acres) served as holding cells for the most murderous machinery of Hitler's extermination "solution" for the Jews. Approximately three-quarters of all the Jews deported to Birkenau were gassed upon arrival. Indeed, Birkenau was the very definition of a death camp: it had its own railway station for transporting prisoners, four huge gas chambers, each of which was capable of gassing 2000 prisoners at a time, and crematoria were outfitted with electric lifts to take the bodies to the ovens.

Visitors can climb to the second story of the principal watchtower at the entrance, from where it is apparent just how vast this camp was. Stretching out are seemingly unending lines of barracks, watchtowers and barbed-wire fences; the camp could hold a total of 200,000 inmates. At the rear of the camp, beyond a grisly pond where the ashes of the murdered were dumped, is an enigmatic monument to the dead of the Holocaust, with inscriptions in the 20 languages of the prisoners who were murdered at Auschwitz and Birkenau.

To get to Auschwitz and Birkenau, you can take a two-hour train or frequent bus (90 minutes; nos. 2-5 or 24-30) leaving from in front of the Kraków train station. However, you will need to take a taxi to Birkenau, as there is no frequent bus service. Alternatively, you could sign up for one of the many package tours offered by any travel agency in Kraków.

ZAKOPANE & THE TATRA MOUNTAINS

Europe's second-largest chain of mountains after the Alps, the Carpathian Mountains (Karpaty) along the southern border of Poland are where many Poles go to play. It is a stunningly beautiful region of forests, lakes, historic mountain towns and spa villages, and terrific hiking and skiing. The High Tatra are the highest range among the Carpathian Mountains, and the most attractive and famous town is Zakopane ("zahk-oh-pahn-ah"), nearly on the border with Slovakia. The town, about 2½ hours south of Kraków, is easily reached by buses that leave frequently from outside the Kraków train station. There are also trains, but they are considerably slower (4 hours).

A small, Alpine-like village, **Zakopane** is undeniably cute, with a terrific backdrop of snow-capped mountains and rustic chalets made of logs. A remote mountain outpost until it began to gain notice in the late 1800s, Zakopane is equally popular for both winter and summer holidays, drawing more than 2 million visitors a year who come here for outdoor sports and chic shopping opportunities. It is also a center of Góral folk art, traditional mountain music, and a unique style of wooden highlander architecture that was elevated to high art in the mid-19th century by several notable artists and architects.

The village's main drag is the pedestrian-only shopping street **Krupówki,** where fashionable visitors parade up and down day and night — it's probably the closest thing to Aspen, Colorado you'll find in Poland. There are several interesting wooden buildings, horse carriages for hire, and sellers of folk art and local snacks. At the lower end of the promenade, the **Tatra Museum** (Muzeum Tatrzánskie, at

Market stalls offering woolen goods on ul. Krupówki in the mountain town of Zakopane, at the foot of the Tatra.

Artistry and creativity live on in the beautifully carved tombstones of Zakopane's old cemetery.

no. 10) houses an interesting collection of local folk art and exhibits on local flora and fauna.

At the end of Krupówki, turn left at ul. Kościeliska. A couple hundred yards or so on the right side is the old parish church (**Stary Kościół**), a splendid, tiny rustic wooden chapel dating to 1847. Next to it is a fantastic old cemetery (**Stary Cmentarz**) populated with a fascinating array of carved wooden tombstones and gravemarkers, echoing the predominant mountain artisanry and often works of incredible creativity. The wooden homes nearby are excellent examples of the "Zakopane style."

Zakopane has earned a reputation as an artists' village, and there are several galleries and small museums of interest. One is the **Władysław Hasior Gallery**, near the train station at ul. Jagiellońska 16; it shows the contemporary works of this artist closely associated with Zakopane.

One of the finest examples of the unique architectural style found in Zakopane is the wooden **Jaszczurówka Chapel** designed by Stanisław Witkiewicz — who is credited with developing the style — in 1908, about 10 km outside of town. It's probably best to take a taxi (and have the driver wait) if you're interested in viewing this handsome high-lander church, perhaps the best of its kind.

At the foot of the Tatra, Zakopane is blessed with one of the most spectacular landscapes in Poland. Even if you haven't come to ski, it's fun and worthwhile to take the cable car up to **Mt. Kasprowy** for the splendid views of the mountains, hiking trails, and ski slopes above the town. The cable car ride, about 25 minutes long with a stop and

Mt. Kasprowy Wierch in the Tatra range offers delightful views, and bountiful slopes and trails for skiers.

transfer at an intermediate station, takes you (and crowds of skiers in winter) up to the summit of Mt. Kasprowy Wierch, at 1,985 m (6512 ft). There you can stand with one foot in Poland, the other in Slovakia. Return cable car tickets (28 zł) give you a mandatory 1 hour and 40 minutes at the top, so if you don't have skis or don't plan to hike, you might want to bring a book. In summer, many people take the ride up and walk back down along a series of marked trails (about 2 hours). To get to the cable car station in

Zamość was intended to be the perfect city — and it is still charming after hundreds of years.

Kuźnice (south of Zakopane), take a taxi, bus no. 7 from directly in front of the bus station, or a minibus across the street from the bus stop.

If you're interested in hiking excursions in the area, including everything from easy walks through valleys to hardcore Tatra excursions to beautiful lakes, inquire at the rustic-looking tourism office at Kościuszki 17, near the bus station. The Tatra are for serious mountaineers only, and require special equipment and preferably a guide. Less taxing nature spots suitable for day-long hiking destinations include the valleys Dolina Białego, Dolina Strążyska, Dolina Chochołowska, and Dolina Kościeliska.

MAŁOPOLSKA (LITTLE POLAND)

Małopolska, or "Little Poland," occupies the southeast corner of the country between Kraków and Ukraine. The small and agreeably sleepy town of **Sandomierz** is a handsome former trading port on the banks of the Vistula. One of Poland's most ancient towns, it prospered during the Renaissance. Its old town, on a hill above the river, has a smattering of fine buildings, including the town hall on the Rynek, or main square, a 14th-century cathedral and castle, and St. James's Church, built in 1230. Of particular interest to visitors is the underground route that dips into a couple of dozen cellars beneath the townhouses on the Rynek.

Zamość

The small and occasionally soporific Renaissance town of Zamość is one of Poland's little gems. The old town has more than 100 buildings and monuments of artistic and historic distinction. The city was planned by the politician and nobleman Jan Zamoyski, who sought to build a perfect city, enclosed within fortifications, in the center of the Lublin

Upland. To carry out his plan, Zamoyski commissioned an Italian architect from Padua, Bernardo Morando, in 1580. The town's strategic location on important East-West trade routes resulted in considerable prosperity in the 17th century. Its fortifications were so strong that it was impregnable to the Tartars and Cossacks in the early 17th century, and was one of only three cities in Poland able to resist the Swedish Deluge of 1656.

Zamość's **main square** (Rynek), dominated by a large, pink town hall with a tall Baroque clock tower, is one of Poland's most splendid. To the right of the town hall are richly ornamented and arcaded houses painted vivid green, yellow, brick-red and blue, with Oriental detailing of 17th-century Armenian merchants. The other houses on the remaining three sides of the square are plainer and painted in more subtle pastels, but don't detract from the square's great harmony. On each side of the Rynek are eight houses (save the north side, which is dominated by the town hall).

On the north side of the Rynek is the **Regional Museum** (Muzeum Okręgowe), which houses an array of items ranging from archaeological finds to armaments and religious sculptures, including an interesting clay model of the Zamość old town and paintings of the Zamoyski clan. More importantly, the museum is an opportunity to walk through the interior of two of the grand old burgher houses on the Rynek. Much of the houses' rich detailing — stone carving, frescoes around the top of rooms, and handsome wood-beam ceilings have been well restored.

Just north of the Rynek is the former Jewish Quarter. In its heyday, Zamość was a multicultural city; Jews, Armenians, Germans, Greeks, Turks, Dutch, and Italians all came to the city to trade. The former synagogue here now houses the town library.

The Baroque clock tower is the focal point of Zamość's Renaissance main square, one of Poland's most splendid.

West of the Rynek is the large but rather plain **Collegiate Church**. To its immediate south, the **Religious Museum** (Muzeum Sakralne) is a small, three-room collection of mostly Renaissance religious objects and paintings with curious translations into English like "fourth heir in tail."

On the eastern edge of Old Town is the one surviving bastion of the seven that once formed the massive fortifications surrounding Zamość. The **Lviv Gate,** next to a large and rather uninteresting market, is one of three original entrances to the city. Across from it is the large **Franciscan Church,** which retains none of its Baroque splendor, which was destroyed when occupiers transformed it into a hospital and then military barracks. Today it is little more than a barren shell, though it still packs them in for Mass.

Even though Zamość has been designated a UNESCO World Heritage Site, its citizens don't yet seem accustomed to the curious attentions and cameras of foreign tourists in their midst. That makes it a good place to see a very pretty and exceedingly well-preserved little town where the citizens don't yet all speak English and go about their business with little regard for the *złotys* of outsiders. On the other hand, if you're looking for something to do after taking in the grand main square and handful of streets that define Zamość's relaxed old town, you might be better off moving on to Kraków or Warsaw. If that's the case, there are buses and trains to each, about 5-6 hours to either destination,

Taxis: Word to the Wise

Taxi drivers in Warsaw and many other cities in Poland have a reputation as thieves. Not all of them, of course — just the ones called "mafia taxis," which are not officially registered and either don't have meters or use meters that are rigged to rack up rates at double or triple the normal speed. For the uninitiated, mafia taxis look pretty much like all the others. They have a "TAXI" sign on the roof and wait in official taxi lines at airports and railway stations, seemingly uninhibited by law. It's best to either call for a taxi (even at the airport or train station) or choose one with an identifiable name and myriad telephone numbers on the vehicle.

though the connections from Lublin, just north, are faster and more frequent.

Kazimierz Dolny

The small, charming mercantile town Kazimierz Dolny, perched on the banks of the Vistula, became wealthy from the grain trade in the 16th century. Kazimierz has become a popular day-trip from Warsaw, and is likely to be busy on summer weekends.

The Old Town is notable for several fine burgher's arcaded town houses with elaborate Renaissance stucco work around the Rynek, or main square, which is also distinguished by a central wooden well. Two small museums are worth exploring. The **Silversmithery Museum** has a fine collection of silver work and decorative arts, including many Jewish pieces. Just south of the Rynek, on ul. Senatorska 17, is the fine Celejowska House, in which you'll find the **Town Museum**, a collection of paintings and documents that tell the story of this city, founded by Poland's great builder, Kazimierz the Great, in the 1300s. Jews began to settle the town not long after, and they remained a potent community, eventually growing to more than half of Kazimierz's population.

The ruins of the town's 14th-century castle, a short walk north of the Rynek, provide good panoramic views above the river, though they're better at the watchtower a little farther up the hill and the best at Three Crosses Hilltop — the latter a rather steep climb east of the Rynek. You can reach it returning from the watchtower.

WARSAW (WARSZAWA)

King Sigismund Vasa moved the royal court from the ancient city of Kraków to Warsaw, on the banks of the

River Vistula in the center of the country, in 1609. Though Kraków would remain the cultural and spiritual heart of Poland, the new political and administrative center in Warsaw grew rapidly, adding wide boulevards and palatial residences to the small Old and New Towns. It suffered from repeated invasions, occupations, and destruction, and has had to be rebuilt on several occasions. World War II proved to be even more devastating and tragic than previous conflicts; as the war came to a close, Hitler ordered that the old city be systematically burned, and Warsaw was leveled as if an A-bomb had been detonated on it. Miraculously, it was studiously rebuilt according to old photographs, paintings, and architectural plans.

Though Warsaw is Poland's capital, it doesn't usually prove as captivating to visitors as Kraków or Gdańsk. In part, that's because it's a city in transition, leading the way for the new post-Communist, pre-European Union Poland. Outside the old town, the city is chaotic and unlovely, the architecture a haphazard and sometimes ugly mix of Stalinist concrete blocks, older buildings in need of restoration, and gleaming modern towers, all with little thought given to urban planning. Neighborhoods are somewhat difficult to define. Still, it's a dynamic city of 2 million people with an important Royal Way, stunningly rejuvenated historic center, reminders of the Warsaw Ghetto and monuments of Jewish legacy, and an important cultural nucleus.

Warsaw Tourist Information offices have a brochure to aid your stroll along the Royal Way. Pick up the detailed map, with all the items discussed here and many more enumerated, called "Warsaw: The Royal Way." (See page 79.)

The Vistula divides Warsaw down the middle, but almost everything of interest to visitors is located on the west

Warsaw's Old Town skyline, reconstructed after World War II.

bank. The Royal Way, the focus of most sightseeing, stretches from the Old Town south to Łazienki Park and Wilanów, the king's palace.

Old Town & Market Square

Warsaw's **Old Town** (Stare Miasto) would be remarkable even if it hadn't been rebuilt from scratch after being razed during World War II. How extensive was the annihilation?

Some historians estimate that 85 percent of the Old Town was destroyed. It is impossible not to marvel that in just 10 years after the war, the entire Old Town was resurrected with abundant care for the architecture, aesthetics, and soul of Warsaw. Competition for rebuilding projects was intense, and in fact, many other towns were neglected because of the resources directed to Warsaw. Incredibly, it looks, and more importantly feels, authentic, like a town with a medieval layout and Renaissance façades. The reconstructed city is a true testament to a people who refused to be defeated, even though the city's population had been reduced by more than two-thirds. Even though

Market Square features a pleasing array of merchants' houses with Gothic, Baroque, and Renaissance details.

many of the buildings only date from the mid-1950s, the entirety of the Warsaw Old Town was named to UNESCO's list of World Heritage Sites in 1980.

It's probably best to begin a tour of Warsaw at the entrance to Old Town, **Castle Square** (Plac Zamkowy). A tall column with a bronze **statue of King Sigismund** — who moved the capital to Warsaw — marks the square, against a backdrop of vibrantly colored pastel town houses with red tile roofs. The fortifications that once enclosed the Old Town were dismantled in the 19th century, though you can still see fragments of them on one side of the square.

On the eastern side of the square is the massive **Royal Castle** (Zamek Królewski). Though a fortress was first established on this spot in the 1300s, the present structure is, like the whole of its surroundings, a recent 20th-century reconstruction. In 1944, it was little more than a smoking pile of rubble, with all its great interiors destroyed by bullets, dynamite, and fire. Almost all the royal collection of great works of art and tapestries was stolen or destroyed, though it should be noted that

> Secessionism was a local form (spreading east from Germany and Austria) of early 20th-century art and architecture that was tied to Art Nouveau. In Austria and Germany it was called Jugensdstil, in Spain modernismo, and in Poland and Hungary, Secessionism. (See page 41)

many pieces, including furnishings, were removed for safekeeping when the war broke out. Reconstruction did not begin until 1971, and the Castle was reopened to the public in 1984…Voilà! An 18th-century castle! As they pass through the stately rooms with excellent stucco detailing and lush works of art (most of which are copies of originals), visitors to the Castle have to keep reminding themselves of the fact that what they are seeing was rebuilt in its entirety in the past 30 years.

Fragments of original building materials, including carvings and stucco pieces, were used in every possible case, and it is frequently possible to distinguish what is new from what is original if you look hard enough.

The Royal Castle was the official residence of the kings of Poland from the 17th century on, and it is where Poland's landmark Constitution — the second oldest in the world, after the United States — was passed by the Sejm (parliament). The Castle interior is visited according to two routes, for which there is normally separate admission. Route I takes in the ground-level courtiers' lodgings, parliamentary chambers, Prince Stanisław's

The Royal Castle is fraught with a rich and complex history that dates back to the 1300s.

apartment, and the Jan Matejko rooms. Route II visits the upper-level Great and King's apartments. Each tour is estimated to take about an hour; if you must choose, you should probably opt for Route II, which covers the true highlights of the Castle.

The **King Stanisław August apartments** are among the most opulent rooms in the castle. On the upper level, the massive, mid-18th-century Ballroom — used variously as a concert hall, meeting and audience room, and the first room to be destroyed in 1939 — is perhaps the most stunning of all the rooms. Note the perfectly named ceiling painting (a reconstruction), "The Dissolution of Chaos." The **Canalletto Room** shows off detailed paintings of Warsaw's Old Town architecture, by the Italian Bernardo Bellotto, which survived the war and were instrumental in the capital's reconstruction efforts. In the **Marble Room**, another highlight, you'll see portraits of the 22 kings of Poland. The **Throne Room** glitters with a red-and-gold canopy of handmade silver-embroidered eagles. The originals were stolen by the Germans, but one eagle was recovered in the U.S. in 1991. It was bought by the Castle, and from it the entire canopy was reconstructed.

Sunday visits to the Royal Castle, from 11am-4pm, feature a single route that includes the most attractive parts of Routes 1 and II. Even better, the visit is free on Sunday. Guided visits for groups (extra charge) are available every day but Sunday, however.

You can also visit the very interesting **Castle Cellars**, where an exhibition of remnants recovered from excavations in the Old Town is displayed, with any ticket.

From Plac Zamkowy, head north along ul. Świętojańska. On the right is **St. John's Cathedral** (Archikatedra Św. Jana), the oldest in Warsaw, from the 14th century. The cathedral was largely leveled during the war; though the Gothic brick exterior was rebuilt, too much of the interior was lost, and the Cathedral now looks wholly different than it did when the last king of Poland, Stanisław August Poniatowski, was crowned

> **The Warsaw Tourism Office distributes an excellent pamphlet, "Historical Sites of Jewish Warsaw," that describes and maps out 29 monuments and places of interest commemorating the Jewish community of Warsaw, making it easy for those with a special interest to follow the route. (See page 85.)**

and buried here. The crypt holds the tombs of several famous Poles, among them the dukes of Mazovia, the Nobel Prize-wining writer Henryk Sienkiewicz, and first president of Poland, Gabriel Narutowicz. St. John's was a protagonist during the 1944 Warsaw Uprising against the German occupiers. German tanks even entered the confines of the church. If you walk around the outside to the south wall, you'll see lodged in the stone actual fragments of the heavy equipment used by the Nazis to tear down the Old Town.

Head a little farther north to the heart of the Old Town, the lively **Market Square** (Rynek Starego Miasta). The compact square is perhaps Poland's finest, an unusually harmonious colorful ensemble of mostly four-level 16th–18th-century (style) merchants' houses with wonderful Gothic, Baroque, and Renaissance details. And it's simply an amazing rebuilding story; it's hard to believe the square is a replica of what stood here before the war. In the center of the Rynek are two water pumps and a statue of Syrena, the Warsaw mermaid of ancient legend. The square is popular with visitors, who frequent the roster of excellent, if expensive, restaurants that inhabit the ground floors and cellars of several of the town houses.

The imposing Barbican stands over a moat at what used to be the northern gate of the city, now the edge of the New Town.

On the north side of the Rynek is the rambling **Historical Museum of Warsaw** (Rynek Starego Miasta 42). A documentary film, "Warsaw Will Never Forget," shows the extent of the wartime destruction and efforts to rebuild the city (Tues-Sat, 12pm; in English). The rest of the museum sprawls among four floors and some 60 rooms of a large town house, taking the kitchen-sink approach to telling the complicated story of the city's history (i.e., everything's historical, so put it all on display). There are city drawings and engravings, a sizeable exhibit on recent archaeological excavations, an interesting mock-up of an 18th-century burgher's house, armaments, documents of the resistance movement, Nazi uniforms, and much more. The museum is an unending labyrinth, with most explanations in Polish only, and guards will make you follow its trajectory in an order that only makes sense to them.

Beyond the Market Square the cobblestone streets lead to attractive little corners, quiet courtyards, and tight passageways. It's a great place to wander, day or night, though you should of course exercise caution after dark. Don't miss the area behind the cathedral, where you'll find a small, pretty square (Kanonia) and a terrace with views across the Vistula. Northwest of the Rynek, on ul. Podwale, is a **Monument to the Little Insurgent,** a bronze statue of a small boy hidden under a giant military helmet and carrying an automatic rifle, a symbol of the young children who fought alongside adults in the 1944 Warsaw Uprising against the Nazis. North of the Market Square, ul. Nowowiejska leads to defensive walls, largely rebuilt, and the semicircular Gothic Barbican, standing over a moat at what was the northern gate to the city.

Trains from Warsaw to Gdańsk do not leave, as you might expect, from the "Warszawa – Gdańsk" station serving the northern route. Instead, they depart from Centralna Station. (See page 88.)

Beyond the Barbican is the **New Town** (Nowe Miasto), where Warsaw expanded after outgrowing the walled Old Town in the 15th century. The two parts were not officially linked until the 18th century. Since it was created as a separate town, New Town not only has a similar layout to the Old Town, it has its own parish church and town hall. There are a half dozen churches in New Town, including the Baroque **Church of the Nuns of the Holy Sacrament** (Kościół Sakramentek), on the **New Town Square** (Rynek Nowego Miasta).

Look also for the **Maria Skłodowska-Curie Museum** (ul. Freta 16), just down the street from the Barbican. Madame Curie, as she's better known, was born here in Warsaw, though she lived most of her adult life in France. A scientist and physician, she was the first woman to teach at the Sorbonne in Paris. She discovered radium and polonium — and the phenomenon of radioactivity — and won the Nobel Prize in 1903 (for physics) and in 1911 (for chemistry).

When you need a break, consider that New Town is also known for its restaurants.

The Royal Way

The Royal Way is the elegant four-km (2.5-mile) trajectory along which the Polish monarchy would travel south from their official residence, the Royal Castle, to the summer palace, Łazienki. The route is lined with palaces, churches, town houses, museums, and monuments along or just off the main streets Krakowskie Przedmieście, Nowy Świat, and Aleje Ujazdowskie.

The Teatr Wielki, Poland's National Opera House — only its façade survived the bombing of World War II.

Krakowskie Przedmieście is the first stretch of the route and one of Warsaw's classic streets. **St. Anne's Church** (on Krakowskie Przedmieście 68) was built in the mid-15th century, then rebuilt in the Baroque style after marauding Swedes burned it. One of the few major churches to avoid devastation in World War II, its observation tower has great views of the Royal Castle and Old Town. If you wish to take an immediate detour, walk a couple of blocks west along Senatorska to Pl. Teatralny, which is dominated by the grand **Teatr Wielki National Opera House,** Poland's greatest opera and ballet institution, built in 1833 by an Italian architect. It was heavily bombed during the second World War, and only its façade survived the blasts.

Back on Krakowskie Przedmieście, as you head south, you'll pass a **statue of Adam Mickiewicz,** Poland's revered romantic poet, and the **Carmelite Church and Shrine.** Farther south is the white Neo-Classical **Radziwiłł Palace,** the residence of the president of Poland. Out front are four stone lions and a statue of Prince Józef Poniatowski, the 19th-century commander-in-chief of the Polish army during Napoleon's Duchy of Warsaw. Across the street is the **Potocki Palace,** now housing the Ministry of Arts and Culture, as well as a gallery of contemporary art. Past the grand Bristol Hotel, built at the turn of the 20th century, is the Baroque **Church of the Nuns of the Visitation,** with a monument to Cardinal Stefan Wyszyński, the Primate of Poland.

West of the Royal Way, in the midst of Ogród Saski gardens, is the **Tomb of the Unknown Soldier** (on Pl. Piłsudskiego). It is housed within the surviving fragments of the 17th-century Saxon Palace — the tomb, placed here in 1925, was the only section of the palace to survive Nazi bombing. The noted British architect Sir Norman Foster has been commissioned to redesign this desolate feeling square.

South of Potocki Palace, **Warsaw University** is denoted by massive, handsome gates atop which perches the traditional Polish eagle. It is the capital's top institution of higher learning, in perpetual rivalry with Kraków's Jagellonian University. Several of the buildings are downright palatial; the oldest dates to 1634. The **Church of the Holy Cross,** across the street from the university, is a mausoleum of sorts for famous Poles, among them one of the most famous in history, the composer Frédéric Chopin. In fact, in accordance with his will, only his heart is here, in an urn; the rest of his remains lie in France.

The statue at a fork in the road is one of Poland's other most famous sons, the great astronomer **Nicholas Copernicus** (Mikołaj Kopernik). With his theory of a heliocentric universe, Copernicus, as Poles commonly say, "stopped the sun and moved the earth." The boulevard at this point becomes **Nowy Świat,** one of Warsaw's most fashionable, and is lined with chic boutiques and cafés. Like the Old Town, this street was almost wholly destroyed during the war.

Set a couple of blocks back from Nowy Świat is Ostrogski Palace, which is the site of the **Frédéric Chopin Museum** (take Świętokrzyska to Tamka streets). This lovely palace is full of artifacts and memorabilia from the life of this outstanding classical composer. Nearby are several other terrific palaces, the Zamoyski Palace (on ul. Foksal), Przezdziecki Palace, and Branicki Palace (ul. Smolna).

The **National Museum** (Muzeum Narodowe), on the busy cross street Al. Jerozolimskie 3, holds a huge collection of art — everything from Roman and Egyptian archaeology and medieval art to antique furniture and large galleries of Polish and European painting. Ujazdowskie Avenue is lined with embassies in elegant palaces, and nearby are the Sejm (Polish Parliament) and a pair of attractive

parks, Ujazdowski and Łazienkowski, the latter especially esteemed by Varsovians.

Łazienki Palace

The splendid **Łazienki Palace and Garden Complex** (Łazienki Królewskie) is the former summer residence of King Stanisław August Poniatowski, Poland's final monarch. At the time of its construction in 1793, the "Palace on the Water" was far removed from the capital. Today, though, the 74-hectare (183-acre) park, opened to the public in 1818, lies right on the fringes of downtown Warsaw. The original 17th-century thermal baths were reshaped by the Italian architect Dominic Merlini into a magnificent classical palace. Other buildings, including a theater and the White House (Biały Dom) villa, along with several pavilions, orangeries, paths, and canals, were added, transforming the complex into a mix of French classical and Baroque architecture and English-style gardens. The peaceful park is a favorite strolling ground of many denizens of the capital.

In the main building, the Palace on the Island, the Neo-Classical Ballroom, Salmon Room, and Art Gallery, which once displayed some 2500 works of art (the most valuable of which were stolen or destroyed, though it still contains pieces from the collection of Stanisław August), are especially notable, as is the Dining Room, where the king held his famous "Thursday dinners" with cultural and political figures. In the Bacchus Room, the original Delft tiles are all unique.

At the opposite end of the park, overlooking the Vistula Escarpment, is a recreation of the 1926 Secessionist **Monument**

The Łazienki Palace and Gardens Complex awaits as a magnificent destination on the fringes of Warsaw.

to Frédéric Chopin, depicting the composer under a willow tree, which is made to look like his piano-playing hand. The monument — which was reportedly the first destroyed by the Nazis — forms a popular outdoor recital hall for summer concerts.

Wilanów

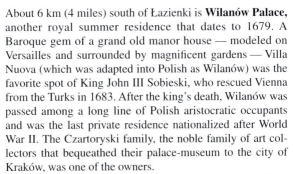

About 6 km (4 miles) south of Łazienki is **Wilanów Palace,** another royal summer residence that dates to 1679. A Baroque gem of a grand old manor house — modeled on Versailles and surrounded by magnificent gardens — Villa Nuova (which was adapted into Polish as Wilanów) was the favorite spot of King John III Sobieski, who rescued Vienna from the Turks in 1683. After the king's death, Wilanów was passed among a long line of Polish aristocratic occupants and was the last private residence nationalized after World War II. The Czartoryski family, the noble family of art collectors that bequeathed their palace-museum to the city of Kraków, was one of the owners.

Even though many of the most valuable works of art were either stolen or destroyed, the palace, which didn't suffer great damage during World War II, still contains one of the largest collections of Polish portraits from the 16th to 19th centuries. The ground floor of the palace is the most opulent; the Great Crimson Room is a dining hall disguised as a painting gallery. After your tour, be sure to walk around the Italian gardens, noticing the palace's fine Baroque exterior decoration, the Anglo-Chinese park, and the pond and Roman bridge. Near the entrance to the palace grounds, somewhat incongruously, sits the **Poster Museum** (Muzeum Plakatu), dedicated to the fine art of Polish poster art, a medium still highly respected today.

Jewish Warsaw

Thousands of Jews arrived in Warsaw in the second half of the 14th century, though they were expelled by royal decree not long thereafter. They were finally allowed to settle in the city again in 1768, and by the start of World War II, approximately 350,000, or 30%, of Warsaw's citizens were Jews. It was at that time the largest Jewish community in pre-war Europe. The residential Jewish Quarter, around the Mirów and Muranów districts (between the Palace of Culture and Science and the Jewish Cemetery in

The Wilanów Palace houses one of the largest collections of 16th–19th-century Polish portraits.

the northwest corner of the city), was transformed into a ghetto by the Nazis. After the Warsaw Uprising in 1943, German troops torched the ghetto.

Today only about 2,000 Jews live in Warsaw. The most obvious reminders of the former Jewish presence are the dilapidated buildings on **ul. Próżna.** A Jewish foundation has been entrusted with the restoration of these buildings, but for the time being they are poignant reminders of devastation. The **Nożyk Synagogue** (ul. Twarda 6), still in use, is the only surviving Jewish house of prayer in the city. Another haunting symbol of Jewish martyrdom is the fragment of the **Ghetto Wall** (ul. Sienna 55), constructed in 1940.

> Fans of the German writer Günter Grass, winner of the 1999 Nobel Prize for Literature, may want to visit the suburb that features in several of his novels. You can take a train to Wrzeszcz and see, for example, the grocery store at ulica Lelewela, which appears in several works by Grass (who was born in Gdańsk in 1927).

Farther north, the **Jewish Cemetery** (Cmentarz Żydowski), which abuts the Powązkowski Cemetery (see below) and was founded in 1780, gives the overpowering impression of neglect: Many of the 150,000 tombstones are toppled over and branches have grown over the tops of them. It seems a shame, but you quickly realize that the Jewish population of Warsaw (and indeed, Poland) was decimated during the war, and most of the people buried here in all probability simply have no family to care for the gravesites. A monument at the **Umschlagplatz,** on ul. Stawki, marks the spot where 300,000 Jews were transported by train from the ghetto to the Treblinka concentration camp.

On ul. Zamenhofa, the **Monument to the Heroes of the Ghetto** is a tribute to the poorly armed but valiant Jews who rose up against their Nazi oppressors in 1944. The monument, in the spot where the month-long fighting was heaviest, is a bas-relief that incorporates stone that had been ordered by the Third Reich to commemorate its planned victory.

West of Old Town, the **Powązkowski Cemetery** (Cmentarz Powązkowski) is Warsaw's oldest, largest, and most spectacular necropolis, with a host of Warsaw's and Poland's most distinguished citizens, from presidents to poets, in their final resting places. The cemetery is jam-packed with tombstones and mausoleums of all shapes and sizes, many obvious testaments to the wealth and prestige of those they shelter. Some are grand, some restrained, some crowned by beautifully expressive sculpture, but all are covered by a fuzzy light green moss.

Warsaw's **New City Center,** near the central train station (Warszawa Centralna), roughly equidistant between Old Town and Łazienki Park, is a chaotic commercial area, teeming with banks, hotels, shops, and thick traffic. It's perhaps most notable for the presence of a building that has become a symbol of the city, despite being abhorred by almost all Varsovians. The **Palace of Culture and Science,** a 1955 Stalinist

Warsaw's oldest and largest cemetery is, not surprisingly, also its most dramatic.

monstrosity that was ostensibly a gift of the Russian government to the Polish people, is Warsaw's tallest building, at 231 m (758 ft). Inside are many shops and galleries, and an observation deck on the 30th floor affords views of the entire city and surrounding Mazovian plains — when not obscured by smog. There has been much public hand-wringing over what to do with the rude pile, an unpopular reminder of life under the Soviets. Many have argued for its destruction or exterior remodeling, but it seems any drastic project is simply too expensive and difficult, and most citizens are resigned to living with it. It is part of the capital, though a universally disparaged one.

GDAŃSK

The northern city of Gdańsk catapulted to the world's attention as the focus of struggles between Polish workers and the Communist regime in the early 1980s. Images of the Gdańsk shipyards were beamed into living rooms around the world. The Solidarność, or Solidarity, workers' union not only set in motion a movement that would eventually topple governments throughout the Soviet Union, its leader, Lech Wałęsa — a shipyard electrician — became the first democratically elected president of post-Communist Poland in 1990.

Though Gdańsk 's recent history has grabbed headlines, this city on the Baltic Sea has long been an important, and contentious, place. In 1308, the Teutonic Knights stormed the city, called Danzig by the Germans, and transformed it into their medieval stronghold on the Baltic. It later became a prosperous port and trade center as part of the Hanseatic League in the 14th century. For two centuries, the city essentially operated as an independent city-state. By the 16th century, Gdańsk was the largest city in Poland and the country's dominant international trade center. During the Second Partition of Poland at the end of the 18th century, Prussia annexed the city; Napoleon laid siege to it in 1807 and declared it the Free City of Danzig; and the Congress of Vienna in 1815 returned it to Prussia.

Hitler began his acquisitive rampage here, and the assault on Gdańsk in 1939 began the Second World War. The Old City, a spectacular creation of Gothic-, Baroque- and Renaissance-style architecture with a distinct Flemish aesthetic, was obliterated during the war on a level comparable to Warsaw's destruction. The city was meticulously rebuilt, and today it is perhaps the most spectacular of all of Poland's old cities; its Royal Way is breathtaking, even though most of it was reconstructed in the 1950s. Amazingly, Gdańsk looks and feels like a 16th-century city.

Gdańsk is in fact the largest member of a "Tri-City" (Trójmiasto) on the Baltic. Together with Sopot and Gdynia, it forms a 20-km (12-mile) string of independent cities with a common identity along the bay. Gdańsk, still Poland's largest port, is by far the most important and historic of the three, but the other two have become popular resort destinations for Poles and northern Europeans.

The Main Town

Gdańsk is a bit unusual for Polish cities. It has three distinct historic quarters, but the Old Town is not in fact the birthplace of the city, and it also doesn't possess the most attractive architectural ensemble. That distinction falls to the **Main Town** (Główne Miasto).

The Royal Way

Gdańsk, despite its tortuous history of shifting allegiances, was loyal to the Polish crown for three centuries. When the king would travel from the capital, Warsaw, to the largest port (and provider of tax income), he would enter Gdańsk through a series of formal gates and down the extraordinary main thoroughfare. Kraków and Warsaw also have Royal Ways, both of which are longer, but neither is as stunningly picturesque and elegant as the one in Gdańsk. It is one of the undisputed highlights of Poland.

The king would first pass through the brick **Upland Gate** (Brama Wyżynna), built at the end of the 16th century, where he was given the keys to the city. Inside the Upland Gate is the **Golden Gate** (Złota Brama), a considerably more ornamental structure formed by an arch topped by allegorical figures. The gate was added in 1644 but only recently fully restored to its original splendor (minus the gilding that gave the gate its name). Royal processions would then proceed onto **Long Street** (ulica Długa), a pedestrian-only promenade lined with magnificent, brilliantly colored three- and four-story houses with fine Baroque portals, Gothic moldings, Renaissance façades, coats of arms, and whimsical decorations. Most were rebuilt in their entirety after World War II, which left the promenade in total ruins. A few original details did survive. Pause to admire house numbers 28, 29, 35, and 71. At no. 12 is Uphagen's House and the **Museum of Burgher Interiors,** occupying a splendid 18th-century merchant's house, with displays of textiles and rich period furnishings.

At the end of Long Street is the 14th-century **Town Hall** (Ratusz Głównego Miasta), crowned by a tall spire and life-size golden statue of King Sigismund August. The seat of the municipal government, it is one of the focal points of the Royal Way. The opulently decorated interior, rich with oil paintings and frescoes, houses the **Gdańsk History Museum,** where you'll find an outstanding collection of photographs of the city before and after the Second World War. The fabulous Red Room, which once held Council debates, is all original; its decorative elements were dismantled and hidden during the war. Don't miss the views of the city from the second floor of the tower.

Just in front of Town Hall is the **Neptune Fountain**, a Flemish artist's beautiful bronze sculpture of the god of the sea, created in 1549 and converted into a fountain nearly a

Most of the ostentatious homes that line pedestrian-only Long Street had to be rebuilt after the second World War.

century later. It is said to be the oldest secular monument in Poland. Such was the locals' attachment to the fountain that they dismantled it piece-by-piece and hid it during World War II, finally returning it to its original place in 1954. Neptune stands at the head of the second major section of the Royal promenade, **Long Market** (Długi Targ). Several of the most attractive houses in Gdańsk face the long market, which is more a boulevard than a square. Particularly impressive is the mansion **Artus Court** (Dwór Artusa), at no. 46, a former meeting place for Gdańsk merchants, named after the court of King Arthur. Inside the massive hall is an immense mid-16th-century tiled stove, with a stunning assembly of more than 500 decorative tiles. On the same side of the street is the **Golden House** (Złota Kamienica), perhaps the most beautiful in the Old Town. The magnificent façade, thoroughly restored in 2001, is decorated with rich allegorical friezes, busts of historical figures, and at the top, four statues of gesticulating characters from classical mythology.

At the far end of Long Market is the **Green Gate** (Zielona Brama), a massive and bold, four arched structure that is more a building than a gate. In fact, it was intended to be a palace for visiting kings, though the exceedingly cold interior scared them away, and no Polish monarch ever slept at the Green Gate.

Waterfront

Pass through the Green Gate and you'll discover the waterfront of the Motlawa River. The **Great Crane** (Żuraw), the largest in medieval Europe, is a giant gate built in 1444 to lift massive cargo onto ships and install ship masts. The crane now forms part of the sprawling **Central Maritime Museum**, which expands across both sides of the river. It has a collection of antique shipping vessels and boats and, in three restored old granaries across the river, exhibits documenting Polish seafaring history, including Swedish canons from the 17th-century "Deluge." A boat shuttles visitors back and forth across the Motlawa river, and you can also step aboard the Sołdek, Gdańsk's first freight shipper built after WWII.

Return to the interior of the city through **St. Mary's Gate**, a medieval defensive gate, which leads to the quiet but exceedingly evocative cobblestoned street, **Mariacka** (St. Mary's). It is one of the prettiest in Poland, with unique terraces and carved gargoyle drainage pipes emanating from every house. Like others in Gdańsk, this street had to be reconstructed after the war, but it didn't lose any of its charm. Many of the houses are now jewelry shops specializing in amber, the local "semi-precious" stone (it's actually just tree resin).

Neptune Fountain, like most landmarks in Gdańsk and elsewhere in Poland, has its own tumultuous history.

The street terminates in the red-brick Gothic **St. Mary's Church** (Kościół Mariacki). The massive structure, begun in the 14th century but not finished until 150 years later, is one of the

Church and state — the solemn Solidarity monument inside St. Bridget's Church in Gdańsk.

world's largest churches, said to be capable of holding up to 25,000 worshippers. Indeed, it is far more impressive for its sheer size than its exterior beauty. The interior is vast but somewhat plain, a result of war damage. Impressive frescoes were whitewashed. The Gothic vault interior retains 31 chapels, three dozen large windows, and one amazing medieval **astronomical clock.** The 15th-century clock features zodiac signs, phases of the moon, time and date, and a cast of characters that peep out to celebrate the tolling of the hour. Adam and Eve ring the bell, while the 12 apostles emerge from the right side. The clock comes with a cruel twist: It is said that the clockmaker's eyes were put out, by order of the mayor, so that he might never again create a clock to compete with this one.

In the shadow of the St. Mary's behemoth is the **Royal Chapel,** a small 17th-century Baroque Catholic church with a richly ornamented exterior. The dome-topped church was built to comply with the will of the last Primate of Poland. (At the time, Gdańsk was a predominantly Protestant city.)

Another landmark building in Gdańsk Main Town is the **Great Armoury,** at the end of ul. Piwna just west of St. Mary's. Built in 1609 at the edge of the city's medieval walls, it is a huge Renaissance building with a spectacular façade, of obvious Flemish influence. A lot of work went into designing a building that would do little more than store armaments. Restored from WWII damage, it now houses another prosaic creature — a shopping mall. The other side, which faces Targ Węglowy, is less ornate.

At the northern edge of Main Town is **St. Nicholas's Church** (Kościół Św. Mikołaja), wedged into a side street, ul. Świętojańska 72. Unlike much of the city, the Dominican church escaped major war damage. The light interior has a quite stunning collection of 10 black-and-gold Baroque altarpieces affixed to columns on either side of a central nave. It also features a gilded, tiered high altar and impressive Baroque pipe organ. A children's choir sings on Sunday mornings.

Old Town

The **Old Town** (Stare Miasto) developed in tandem with the Main Town, though it was never as rich and after the war was not as lovingly rebuilt. Consequently, it has fewer sights of interest, but enough to warrant a half-day's exploration.

Of principal interest is the **Great Mill**, on ul. Wielkie Młyny, a terrific structure with a sloping tiled roof. Built by the Teutonic Knights in 1350, the mill was the largest in medieval Europe, and it continued to function until the end of World War II. It's a little disappointing, then, to discover that today it houses an indoor shopping mall with all manner of trendy clothing stores. Past the small pond behind the mill and across the street is Gdańsk's **Old Town Hall,** a 16th-century building that was labeled the pearl of the

Dutch Renaissance. Designed by Antoon van Opberghen, who also designed the Great Armoury, this is where the town council met. It now contains a café and exhibition center, but of greatest interest is the rich interior. Simply walk in and take a gander upstairs, where you'll find the Great Hall.

> Crowds gather daily at noon beneath the tower of the Town Hall at Poznań to see two mechanical billy goats emerge from the parapet in the clock tower. A 16th-century tradition, the metal goats butt horns 12 times to signal the hour. (See page 108.)

Directly across the street from the Great Mill is **St. Catherine's Church** (Kościół Św. Katarzyny), the former parish church and the oldest church in Gdańsk, begun in 1220. The Gothic-vaulted interior is most appreciated for the enormous mural, on the left aisle beneath the organ loft, depicting Christ's entry into Jerusalem. The church tower holds a 37-bell carillon that chimes on the hour. Buried in the church is the Polish astronomer Jan Heweliusz.

Directly behind, or east of, St. Catherine's is **St. Bridget's Church** (Kościół Św. Brygidy), which dates to the 15th century but came to prominence recently as a refuge for the Solidarity movement when its leaders were being pursued by the Communist government. Inside are several permanent displays related to human rights struggles of the Polish workers' union. In fact, Lech Wałęsa attended Mass here before he became the spokesman for Solidarność. The politicized nature of the church is evident on the right aisle in a series of crosses from the 1980s strikes, the tombstone of murdered priest (and Solidarność sympathizer) Jerzy Popiełuszko, and a bas-relief history of the workers' union.

A 10-minute walk north takes you to the old Gdańsk ship-yards, where the Solidarity union protests took root. Today the shipyard is quiet, though there's a huge **Monument of the Fallen Shipyard Workers,** an evocative sculpture of crosses and anchors that look like harpoons commemorating the 44 who were killed in the 1970 street riots against the

The awe-inspiring interior of St. Nicholas church was lucky to survive the war without serious damage.

Communists. The monument was unveiled in 1980, at another time of great unrest.

Old Suburb

South of the Main Town is the third component of Gdańsk's historic districts, where the city expanded in the 15th century, now called the **Old Suburb** (Stare Przedmieście). It, too, was devastated during the Second World War, and while the rebuilt neighborhood is largely flavorless, there are a couple of essential sights worth checking out. The neighborhood lies across the major road Podwale Przedmiejskie.

The **National Museum** (Muzeum Narodowe), on ul. Toruńska 1, is one of Poland's most important repositories of medieval art, tapestries, embroidery, gold, and silverware, all housed in a vaulted former Franciscan monastery and hospital. Its most famous work of art is *The Final Judgment*, a colorful triptych by the 15th-century Dutch painter Hans Memling. The Flemish and Dutch collection also contain works by Van Dyck and Breughel the Younger.

Abutting the museum is the **Church of the Holy Trinity** (Kościół Św. Trójcy), the second-largest church in Gdańsk. Built in the 15th century, the Gothic structure has a spacious, whitewashed interior and is remarkably well-preserved. Of particular interest is the high altar, comprising varied panels in a triptych.

EXCURSIONS FROM GDAŃSK

Sopot, a former fishing village just 12 km (7 miles) north of Gdańsk, is one of Poland's most fashionable seaside resorts. It began as a spa town in the 18th century; little damaged by

The brilliance of detail along whimsical Long Street in Gdańsk is not to be overlooked.

World War II, Sopot has a relaxed and elegant feel, complemented by the 19th-century Secessionist buildings. The town of 50,000 balloons with huge crowds of northern Europeans and Poles in summer months, drawn to its chic cafés and restaurants along Bohaterów Monte Cassino, and its sandy beaches and waters in the Gdańsk Bay (finally declared safe for swimming a few years ago). It is perhaps best known, however, for its celebrated nightlife. Sopot also has a 10-km (6-mile) path that runs through the park along the ocean, ideal for walking, running, or cycling. Also popular are the promenade along the 1920s **pier** (Molo Poludniowe), the longest in Poland, and the open-air **Forest Opera House** (Opera Leśna), a delightful amphitheater setting in the woods.

The next, and considerably larger, town north along the bay (21 km/13 miles from Gdańsk), **Gdynia** is also a former fishing village, though in the 20th century it transformed itself into a large and wealthy industrial port city. Gdynia sports a full roster of chic boutiques, bars, restaurants, and museums, which draw visitors from across Poland. Most sights, clustered around the pier, are related to the sea and sailors. Visit the ship museums (the *Błyskawica* and *Dar Pomorza*) at the pier, spend a couple of hours at the **Oceanographic Museum & Sea Aquarium** (Al. Zjednoczenia 1), or pop into the **Navy Museum** (ul. Sedzickiego 3), a museum of Polish warfare.

Both Sopot and Gdynia are easily reached by train (leaving every 10 minutes) from the Gdańsk Główny Train Station.

Anyone looking to escape the crowds of this part of the Bay of Gdańsk should head to the tranquil **Hel Peninsula,** which stretches like a slim finger 35 km (20 miles) across the bay. The string of quiet fishing villages and sandy beaches is gaining in popularity as a serene retreat and an easy day trip from Gdańsk, Sopot, or Gdynia. Trains to Hel (!) leave from Gdynia, and take 2 hours.

Malbork Castle (Marienburg)

Poland's largest and most famous castle, is 60 km (37 miles) south of Gdańsk. The 14th-century medieval fortress, built by the Teutonic Knights on the banks of the River Nogat, gives every impression of being impregnable. It is a monumental complex in red brick, with turrets, drawbridges, and the most solid of walls dominating the flat plains around it — the stuff of fairy tales.

> **During summer months, Malbork Castle stages hour-long evening *son et lumière* shows in the main courtyard.**

In 1280, the Teutonic Knights built a fortified monastery, and in 1308, the Grand Master came to live in Malbork, elevating the status of the settlement to headquarters of the entire Order. The interior of the castle is astounding, a veritable labyrinth of unending rooms and chapels. Highlights include the perfectly harmonious vaulting in the refectory, the stunning Gothic portal known as the Golden Gate, the massive Knight's Hall, and the museum collection of amber. Even after the defeat and retreat of the Teutonic Knights, the castle never fell into ruin. It became a residence of the Polish monarchs.

Visits are by guided tour only, though some parts of the castle complex can be visited on one's own. Getting to Malbork is straightforward: The train journey from Gdańsk Główny station takes 40 minutes by express train or an hour by regular train. From the town of Malbork, the castle is an easy 10-minute walk. It's well worth the time to visit this impressive landmark.

TORUŃ

In the lower Vistula Valley, directly south of Gdańsk, lies the handsome and historic city of Toruń. Founded by the Teutonic Knights in 1233, the medieval walled town sits on the right bank of Poland's greatest river; its positioning allowed it to rise to prominence in the 14th and 15th centuries as a Hanseatic port city. It's probably best known, however, as the birthplace of Mikołaj Kopernik — or, as most people know him, Nicholas Copernicus, the great 16th-century astronomer.

Toruń's city council outlawed wooden buildings in the 14th century, requiring all the city's important edifices to be made of brick and stone. At the time, the city won accolades as "beautiful red Toruń." With a unique collection of Gothic architecture, including a castle, fine churches, fortifications,

a leaning tower, and the home of Copernicus, Toruń is distinguished as a proper UNESCO World Heritage Site. Today, the historic center is a living museum of architecture, but can feel like a slightly sleepy, one-astronomer town.

Old Town

In the center of the historic center (Stare Miasto) is the **Old Town Square** (Rynek Staromiejski). In its middle stands the dignified **Town Hall** (Ratusz), a solid Gothic brick construction raised in the 14th century and Dutch

Toruń's best-known resident, Copernicus, in front of the Town Hall.

NICOLAUS COPERNICUS

Renaissance turrets and gables (the clock tower, formerly an independent structure, was built in 1247). Suitable for a town known for a mathematician-astronomer, the Town Hall has 12 halls representing the months of the year, 52 small rooms representing the number of weeks, and 365 windows for each day of the year. The former municipal seat of government has been almost wholly taken over by the **Regional Museum** (Muzeum Okręgowe), which displays an impressive collection of Gothic art, stained glass, and Polish painting. Climb to the top of the clock tower for a sweeping view of Toruń's red-tile roofs and the river. Down below, two bars inhabit the atmospheric cellars.

In the southeast corner of the square, in front of the Town Hall, is a statue commemorating Toruń's most famous citizen, **Copernicus**. Across the street is a large, extravagant 19th-century building known as **Arthur's Court** (Dwór Artusa), formerly a meeting place for town merchants and today the site of a cultural center. Facing the square on its east side is a pretty yellow four-story building with an ornate Baroque façade and gabled roof. Called the **"House Under the Star"** (Pod Gwiazda), it functions as a very modest museum (Muzeum Okręgowe) with a hard-to-define mission (it recently showed a few posters and other graphic designs). It's worth checking out, though, if only to see its lush interior, which features painted ceilings and the fabulous 17th-century carved-wood spiral staircase that rises three floors.

> While Toruń is still known for its traditional gingerbread, bakers nowadays get pretty creative with the medieval recipe. Look for gingerbread figures of favorite son Copernicus, among other whimsical creations.

On the opposite, or west, side of the Rynek is the rather unimpressive 18th-century **Church of the Holy Spirit.** Between it and the Town Hall is a curious fountain featuring a slew of frogs and a young boy playing the violin. It represents a legend of a frightening moment when Toruń was invaded by frogs and the boy charmed them back to the woods with nothing but the tunes from his violin. Just removed from the northwest corner of the square is the imposing **St. Mary's Church,** a Franciscan monastery from the 13th century. The highlight of the interior is a series of very interesting and colorful frescoes on the columns supporting the nave.

Around the corner (north) is Toruń's **Planetarium,** the most modern in Poland and installed in a 19th-century gasworks, whose round shape was perfect for its needs. There are afternoon shows daily, though the soundtrack is in Polish. Across the street is Toruń's respected Mikołaj Kopernik University, also a feast of Gothic brick; its **Collegium Maius** dates from the end of the 16th century.

Toruń's other major sights are south of the Rynek. On ul. Kopernika is the **Copernicus Museum** (Muzeum Kopernika), which inhabits the handsome burgher house where young Nicholas was born in 1473. The museum has a first edition of his seminal work *De Revolutionibis* along with mostly reproductions of the great scientist's instruments, and it also features a very interesting sound-and-light show of Toruń in the 15th century. Directly south of the museum, along ul. Bankowa, are remnants of the city's fortifications. Although good portions of the walls were destroyed during the 17th-century "Swedish Deluge," and other sections were torn down to allow the city to expand, four bastions and three gates survive. Nearby are old granaries, the Monastery Gate, and the **Leaning Tower.** This last item is curious indeed; it bends noticeably in toward the street. Its structural flaw is explained away by a legend that states that a Teutonic Knight, a monk sworn to chastity, was caught *in flagrante* with a townswoman and made to build a leaning tower to show the harm of deviance from upright moral standards.

On the corner of Żeglarska (where many fine merchant houses were built) and Św. Jana is Toruń's largest church, the **Cathedral of SS John the Baptist and John the Evangelist** (Katedra Św. Janów). The immense brick church took a couple of hundred years to complete. Before going in, note the clock on the southern side; added in the 15th century, it still functions today. The spacious whitewashed interior has Gothic vaulting and a series of attractive chapels and altars. Some frescoes have been uncovered; the most interesting is the monochromatic painting of the devil high at the back of the right aisle. A chapel nearby holds a medieval font in which Copernicus was baptized.

Southwest of the cathedral, at the end of ul. Mostowa, is the **Bridge Gate,** where a bridge over the Vistula — the second in Poland — existed from the end of the 15th century until the early 1800s. Nearby are the ruins of the **Teutonic Castle,** built by the Order in the 13th century. Toruń citizens destroyed it in 1454 (and herded the Order out of town) and it has lain in ruins since. There is just one surviving tower and a covered passageway you can walk through. You'll have to use your imagination to conjure an image of 15th-century Torun with a massive stronghold overlooking the river.

New Town

In contrast to the Old Town, the buildings in the expansion west were constructed mostly of wood. They didn't survive, so what remain in the New Town are predominantly brick constructions of the 15th and 16th centuries.

The outdoor Ethnographic Museum of Toruń comes to life each year as a living reminder of Polish history.

The **New Town Square** (Rynek Nowomiejski) is less impressive than its older counterpart, but it's worth a quick look around. The major church in this part of town is **St. James's Church,** notable for its flying buttresses — unusual for Poland. Inside are some interesting Gothic wall paintings.

Walk west to Plac Teatralny, at the edge of Old Town, where you'll find Toruń's major theater, the Neo-Baroque **Teatr Horzycy**. The park across the intersection holds a very interesting skansen, or outdoor **Ethnographic Museum.** Dating from 1959, it displays a collection of 18th- to early-

20th-century houses that have been moved here from all over the north of Poland. You can wander among them and enter a windmill, fisherman's houseboat from the Vistula river, a blacksmith's shop, and modest farmer's house. Once a year, on a Sunday in September, the skansen becomes a living museum with actors playing the parts of blacksmiths and other rural workers.

POZNAŃ

Halfway between Berlin and Warsaw, Poznań is the principal city of Wielkopolska, a region in western Poland that is one of the country's largest and most historic. Wielkopolska means "Great Poland," a moniker that reflects its role in the development of the Polish nation. Wielkopolska is effectively the birthplace of Poland: in the 10th century, Prince Mieszko succeeded in uniting the Polanie (literally, "people of the fields") and neighboring Slavic tribes, founding the Polish state in 966.

Until the royals adopted Kraków in 1038, Poznań was in essence the capital of Poland. The city began its development on the island of Ostrów Tumski and the new town center was begun in the 13th century. In the 18th century, it fell to the Prussians under the Second Partition and became increasingly Germanic, a trait for which it is known today throughout Poland. In modern times, Poznań is best known for a tragic episode: In 1956, a thunderous workers' strike was crushed by the Communist government, leaving 76 people dead and nearly 1000 injured.

Today Poznań is one of the most dynamic and prosperous cities in Poland, with an attractive historic core, a wealth of Gothic, Renaissance, and Neo-classical architecture, and a civic commitment to business development and international trade fairs. Citizens of Poznań are sometimes chided by other

Poles for being a bit too industrious and money-minded, but their work ethic is the reason the city is second behind Warsaw in terms of international investment. Poznań draws large numbers of business visitors to its fairs that seemingly run all year,

> **Poznań is famous for its St. Martin celebrations, honoring the fourth-century saint, on November 11. On that day, and only that day, Poznańians gobble up St. Martin croissants, in the shape of buffalo horns, stuffed with poppy seeds and almonds.**

but the city also enchants leisure-minded visitors, who concentrate on three primary areas: the Stary Rynek, or Old Town Square, the Ostrów Tumski island, and the New Town (City Center).

Old Market Square

In Poznań you will find the **Old Market Square** (Stary Rynek) one of the largest and finest in Poland. The fairytale **Town Hall** (Ratusz), a fanciful construction of Italian Renaissance designed by Giovanni Battista di Quadro, replaced the original, smaller Gothic 14th-century structure, which was destroyed by a devastating fire in 1536. The building, constructed in the 1550s, features a splendid three-story Renaissance, arcaded loggia and a classical tower, added in 1783, topped by the Polish eagle. The brilliant colors of the frieze above the loggia, depicting the Jagiellonian dynasty kings, have recently been restored to their original splendor, returning the building to its status as one of the most distinctive in Poland. Adding to the sites of interest, just in front of City Hall is a copy of a 1535 pillory, with a Rococo **Proserpina Fountain** dating from the 18th century.

The Town Hall holds the **History Museum of Poznań** (Muzeum Historii Miasta Poznania). The Great Hall is a spectacular vaulted room with a Renaissance ceiling, rich with stucco decoration, coats of arms, symbols of the heavens, and exotic animals. The museum displays a collection of art, medieval sculpture, distinctive "coffin portraits" (paintings of the deceased attached to their caskets) and Poznań crafts from the 10th to the mid-20th century. In the Court Chamber, there are frescoes representing the four continents — Europe, Asia, Africa, and America. Interestingly enough the vaulted Gothic cellars survive from the original town hall.

The old world charm of Poznań's historic quarter resonates in this view from the Town Hall.

Adjoining the Town Hall to the south is a row of narrow and colorful fish sellers' houses, built in the 1500s. Lining the four sides of the square are elegant and colorful arcaded burgher's houses and two magnificent palaces. Many remarkable edifices had to be rebuilt in the 1950s, after WWII, to their original Gothic, Baroque, and Renaissance designs. Almost all of the Rynek's houses have vaulted medieval cellars, several of which have been converted into atmospheric restaurants. Some of the best preserved include no. 37, today the Maison de la Bretagne, but formerly the oldest pharmacy in Poznań — and nos. 40, 41, 42 and 43. No. 41 is a still extant pharmacy established in 1564, the "White Eagle." On the façade of the house of no. 84, today the Henryk Sienkiewicz Literature Museum, you'll see a statue of the Italian architect, Battista di Quadro, who lived in this house while building Town Hall

The 18th-century **Działyński Palace,** at the corner of ul. Frańciszkańska on the west side of the square, is a lovely classical structure painted a light shade of green and decorated with sculptures and reliefs. On top is a pelican, symbolic of Poznań's rebirth after the Partition of Poland. More spectacular than the façade is the Red Room, where "literary Thursdays" were held in the period between the World Wars. The palace at no. 91 belonged to the Miełżyński family.

The **Museum of Musical Instruments,** the only one of its kind in Poland, is housed in no. 45 on the square. Inside you'll discover early phonographs, church and Polish-army drums, a Celtic horn, 17th-century Polish violins from Groblicz, and a piano forte once played by Chopin, as well as odd Polish folk instruments and exotic drums from around the world. The museum is an unusual and fun attraction.

The middle of the square is also occupied by two large, incongruous, and unlovely 1950s- and 1960s-era pavilions, constructed after the war on the sites of the old cloth hall and arsenal. One houses a military museum, the other a contemporary art gallery. They mar the exquisite harmony that would otherwise exist in the square, and while there have been discussions in the municipal government about tearing them down or adding façades more consistent with the Renaissance appearance of the square, any such action is unlikely.

Sandwiched in a passageway between the pavilions and Town Hall is a cute **Monument of a Bamberg Woman** in folkloric dress on the way to a well, with large jugs in both hands. The statue pays tribute to 18th-century immigrants to Poznań from Bamberg, Germany.

One of Poznań's most stately residences is the **Górka Palace,** built in the mid-16th century and occupying an entire block on the corner of Wodna and Świętosławska streets (southeast corner of the Stary Rynek). Note the Renaissance portals; in the interior is a beautiful arcaded courtyard. The palace passed from the Górkas, one of Poznań's most powerful families, to Benedictine nuns during the Reformation; today it is the site of the **Archaeological Museum,** displaying a collection of artifacts dating to the prehistory and foundations of Wielkopolska as well as ancient Egypt. New excavations and restoration are ongoing at the site.

In summer months, the Stary Rynek is full of lively outdoor cafés, and concerts and performances are frequently staged here. At night the square is beautifully illuminated and a wonderful place to take a stroll.

Near Old Town Square

A block south of Górka Palace is Poznań's stunning salmon-colored **Parish Church of St. Stanislaus.** A Jesuit church until 1701, it is one of the most important Roman Baroque churches in Poland. Though not greatly damaged by the war, the Baroque interior, with beautiful stucco work and murals, is in the process of being meticulously restored. Like Michelangelo's Sistine Chapel, its refurbished colors are so bright that the restoration gained detractors. Note the curious flat cupola that is in fact an optical illusion, giving the impression of being a dome. The church organ is an excellent 19th-century example of the work of Friedrich Ladegast.

Adjoining the Parish Church, the handsome orange-pink collection of buildings, formerly the Jesuit College, now house Poznań's municipal government.

West of the Old Town Square are several places of interest. The Baroque **Franciscan Church,** with its twin towers, dates from the first half of the 18th century. The interior features rich stucco work and wall paintings. Across ul. Frańciszkańska is **Przemysław's Castle and Museum of Applied Arts,** featuring historical crafts such as ceramics, glass, and silver. Originally, a true castle stood here in the 13th century, but over the centuries it was continually destroyed and rebuilt. The present building, hardly a castle at all, is a reconstruction from the 18th century.

City Center

Farther west, on Al. Marcinkowskiego, is the **National Museum,** facing Plac Wolności (Freedom Square) — which ought to be called "Bank Square," given the preponderance of Polish and foreign banks here. The main building of the museum is the older one, built at the beginning of the 20th century and modeled on the Berlin Arsenal. The collection of medieval art, 16th-18th century European painting   featuring Spanish and Flemish Old Masters —

and contemporary Polish art, by artists like Malczewski, Matejko, and Wyspiański, is quite impressive. The museum's new wing, opened in 2001, isn't so new at all. It was begun in 1980, which is why, though brand new, it has a dated feel to it. It hosts itinerant exhibitions.

Poznań, in essence the original Polish capital, remains today one Poland's most prosperous cities.

Also on Freedom Square is the **Raczyński Library,** commissioned by a count in the early 19th century and modeled on the Louvre Museum in Paris. It is one of Poland's oldest public libraries.

Architecture from the days of Prussian control of Poznań can be found west of Freedom Square. Look for the colonnaded **Grand Theater** (Teatr Wielki), with a classical portico, and the Neo-Renaissance **Collegium Minus** of the university. In front of the university, in a plaza usually filled with students, is a **Monument to the Victims of Poznań, June 1956,** whose two crosses mourn the 100 protesting workers who were killed in demonstrations against the Communist government.

Across the street is the monolithic **Kaiserhaus,** also called "the castle" by locals, constructed for the German Emperor Wilhelm II (he never once came to spend the night here). The massive structure now holds a cultural center.

Directly west of here is Poznań's international fair grounds, which date to the 1920s and are the biggest and busiest in Poland. A 10-minute walk southwest, down Franklina Roosevelt, past the Poznań Główny Train Station and just on the other side of Głogowska, is **Wilsona Park,** a green space dedicated to U.S. President Woodrow Wilson. Within the park is the **Palm House,** a magnificent greenhouse filled with tropical plants and cacti.

Ostrów Tumski

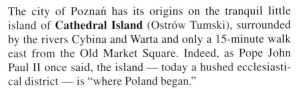

The city of Poznań has its origins on the tranquil little island of **Cathedral Island** (Ostrów Tumski), surrounded by the rivers Cybina and Warta and only a 15-minute walk east from the Old Market Square. Indeed, as Pope John Paul II once said, the island — today a hushed ecclesiastical district — is "where Poland began."

At the beginning of the ninth century, the Piast Dynasty built a settlement and castle on the island. The actual foundations of the pre-Polish state are beneath the Cathedral, the oldest landmark on the island, dating back to 968. An inscription over the main portico reads, "First Episcopal Church in Poland." The main part of the church is Gothic, from the 14th and 15th centuries (the roof, twin towers, and most of the interior were destroyed during World War II). The unusual arcaded gallery above the altar is purely decorative. On the left rear of the altar is the Golden Chapel (Złota Kaplica), a riot of ornate gold decoration from the first half of the 19th century, built as a mausoleum for the two rulers who were instrumental in building the Polish state, Mieszko I and his son, Bolesław the Brave. The chapel on the right aisle has lovely 1616 frescoes on the arches; in the right rear, the Royal Chapel is where the last king buried in Poznań lies (all of the others were subsequently buried in Kraków). The Chapel of the Holy Sacrament holds the impressive Renaissance tomb of the Górka family. Along the aisles is a series of five unique bronze plates, original to the cathedral, which were discovered in 1991 in St. Petersburg's Hermitage Museum and returned to the cathedral.

In the cathedral crypt are the ancient foundations of the first church on this site, excavated in the 1950s, and an archaeological museum. Though the remains of the first two sovereigns of Poland are ostensibly buried here, there's no real proof of that fact.

Across the plaza from the Cathedral is **St. Mary's Church,** a small Gothic church built in the 15th century on the location of the first chapel in Poland (constructed in 950). There are interesting murals lining the interior walls, though the church is not often open to the public.

The Old Town Square in Poznań reflects a city with distinct charm and European flair.

Malta

Poznańians in search of leisure and athletic activities head to Malta — a lake and park district east of Old Town, not the country! Lake Maltańskie is an artificial lake constructed in the 1950s, where there are frequent regattas, a beach, and other water sports, in addition to a year-round manmade ski slope and a summer toboggan run. The path around the lake is also popular with runners and cyclists. Concerts and theater performances are held in summer, and there are several good restaurants and one of Poznań's best hotels on the shore of the lake.

EXCURSIONS FROM POZNAŃ

Two popular side trips from Poznań are to a castle and palace in the small towns of Kórnik and Rogalin, respectively. Both can be visited by bus from Poznań, and you can go first to Kórnik and then on to Rogalin without having to double back to Poznań first. However, the visits would be much easier and less time-consuming with your own transport, since buses to Rogalin are infrequent.

The **Kórnik Castle** (about 20 km/12 miles southeast of Poznań) was built by one of Poznań's richest and most powerful families, the Górkas, in the 15th century. The castle's modified appearance both inside and out was effected under the ownership of another important family, the Działyńskis, in the 1800s. Inside, the castle is a museum of their collections of art and military regalia, as well as of their original furnishings. Beautiful hardwood floors and carved wood portals are found throughout. The most surprising aspect of the interior is surely its Moorish Hall, based on the Alhambra palace in Granada, Spain. The castle also features the third-largest library in Poland, with manuscripts dating all the way back to the ninth century. The grounds beyond the castle were established as an arboretum in the 19th century, with over 2,500 species of plants and trees. The grounds are particularly attractive in spring and fall.

Rogalin Palace is set in the small village of the same name, just 13 km (8 miles) west of Kórnik. The 18th-century Baroque palace of Kazimierz Raczyński, the secretary of the king, it is principally noted for its gardens and small museum. Much of the palace today is undergoing a painfully slow restoration (Hitler youth occupied it during the war and trashed it). The right wing of the museum holds a long series of portraits of the Raczyński family as well as a mock-up of the London apartment of Edward, who became a diplomat. Off to the left of the main house is a gallery of "salon paintings," including Polish artists like Wyspiański, Podkowiński and Malczewski, as well as lesser-known Dutch and French artists. One gallery was specially built for Jan Matejko's *Joan of Arc,* an enormous canvas. In the attractive English-style gardens, which lead to an ancient oak forest of more than 1,000 oaks, are three massive oak trees, each about 600 years old. The famous trees were given the names of three dukes — Lech, Czech, and Rus — who founded the Polish, Czech, and Russian nations.

Rogalin Palace, still undergoing a laborious restoration process, is known for its gardens and fine small museum.

WHAT TO DO

SHOPPING

The demise of Communism in 1989 and the move to a free-market economy have had a dramatic impact on Poland as a shopping destination. Drab state-owned stores are a thing of the past. The dollar and mark (and other currencies) don't go as far today as they once did, but foreign visitors and their Polish counterparts can only be pleased with the opening of trade and vastly improved selection of goods on the market. In major cities like Warsaw and Kraków, Poland doesn't lag far behind Western Europe and North America for commercial opportunities. Even with the end of Communism and inflation, Poland remains considerably cheaper than Western European destinations.

Where to Shop

Poland's development of a market economy has produced a proliferation of stores and boutiques, including many imported from Western Europe and North America. You can now buy most Western goods in large and modern department stores, specialty shops, and market stalls.

For folk art and other handicrafts, start at branches of Cepelia stores, a chain of folk art and souvenir shops in large cities. (Occasionally, they go by different names, even though locals invariably call them Cepelia.) For antiques, the dominant player is the Desa chain (though there are many smaller, independent dealers as well). In Kraków and Warsaw, there are numerous branches, all with different stock, so it pays to visit a few if you're looking for a particular item. There are essentially three places in the country for Polish poster art: in Kraków, Galeria Plakatu Kraków (ul. Stolarska 8-10); and in

Warsaw, Galeria Plakatu (ul. Hoża 40) and the Poster Museum (Muzeum Plakatu) at Wilanów Palace.

Specialty shopping markets and unique venues exist in several cities. These include the famous, long-standing **Cloth Hall stalls,** loaded with crafts and amber jewelry, in Kraków; Warsaw's swank, boutique-lined ul. **Nowy Świat; and ul. Mariacka** in Gdańsk's Main town for amber jewelry. Open-air markets and bazaars include: in Warsaw, Dziesięciolecia stadium in Praga, across the river (actually held in a stadium) and Koło Bazaar, in Wola; in Kraków, the traders' market between the train station and the Barbican; and in Gdańsk, Kupcy Dominikańscy (on Pl. Dominikański 1).

Good sources for local shops and markets in Warsaw, Kraków, and Gdańsk are the local editions of the *In Your Pocket* guide, which features individual store listings.

An open-air art gallery takes full advantage of the city walls in Kraków's Old Town.

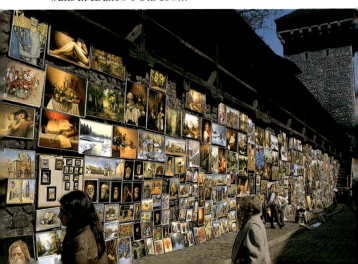

Bargaining is generally only acceptable at the large **open-air markets,** though if you ask for a discount at an antiques store or art gallery, you may very well be granted one.

What to Buy

Amber. Amber is not a semi-precious stone, but a fossilized tree resin. Still, it is very attractive and available in many shades, from yellow to brown, and grades of clarity. The cities near the Baltic Sea, Gdańsk and Gdynia, have an abundance of amber and excellent rosters of shops, often dealing in one-of-a-kind jewelry pieces. Amber is a very popular "stone" in Poland, as well as a popular export. Be careful not to buy amber on the street, as it is likely to be fake; look for a sign of the Amber Association of Poland ("Societas Svccinorvm in Polonia") in shop windows as a guarantee of quality and authenticity.

Art & Antiques. You'll find excellent antique furnishings and religious art throughout Poland, though the best pieces tend to wind up in the wide spectrum of shops and galleries in Warsaw and Kraków, and to a lesser extent cities like Gdańsk and Poznań. Religious icons from the Orthodox Church in Russia can be found, although a large black market in stolen icons exists throughout Central and Eastern Europe, and officials are understandably touchy about their export, even when the item in question is not originally from Poland.

> **Bankomats, or ATM machines, have a reputation for running out of money on weekends and weekdays before work.**

Ceramics & Pottery. Distinctive Kashubian pottery and that known as Ceramika Artystyczna Bolesławiec are sold the world over but are considerably cheaper in Poland. They're not as ubiquitous, though, as one might expect.

Folk Art. Rustic Poland excels at folk art and handicrafts, including hand-carved wooden (usually religious) figures; leather goods from the Tatra mountains; embroidery and lace; hand-painted eggs (especially at Christmas); and colorful naïve art and glass paintings, especially that of Zakopane.

Music. Compact discs from Polish composers are available in record shops in major cities. The most recognizable to Western listeners are composers such as Frédéric Chopin, the father of Polish music, as well as Krzysztof Penderecki and Henryk Górecki, who unexpectedly scored an international best seller with his Symphony No. 3 in the early 1990s. A contemporary film composer, Zbigniew Preisner, who wrote the scores for the Polish director Krzysztof Kieślowski's films, including The Double Life of Veronika, Dekalogue, and the Three Colors trilogy: Red, White, and Blue, is worth seeking out. Of special note is a recording of the best of Preisner recorded live in the Wieliczka Salt Mine outside of Kraków. You can also find recordings of Polish folk music, such as traditional górale tunes from the Tatra highlands.

Poster Art. The art of poster-making for film, theater, and opera is a still thriving and valued art form in Poland, and

---

EXPORTING ART

The export of works of art created prior to May 9, 1945 is officially prohibited in Poland. To do so legally, one must secure permission from the National Museum in Warsaw (Dział Opiniowania Dzieł Sztuki; ul. Myśliwiecka 1, Warsaw) certifying that the piece in question is not of museum quality. However, the process can be costly (a fee of up to 25% of the work's value) and time-consuming, so many visitors understandably decide that it's not worthwhile to have their purchases certified and thus cleared for export.

some of the finest poster artists in the world are Polish, as they have been since the 1950s. You'll find vintage and contemporary posters for familiar Western films and the greatest hits of theater and opera, as well as more obscure titles. Among the stars of contemporary poster art are Górowsky, Stasys, and Sadowski.

Vodka. If you'd like to take back an authentic bottle of Polish vodka, or wódka (pronounced "voot-ka"), look for Wyborowa, Żytnia, or any of the flavored vodkas, such as Żubrówka (with a blade of "bison grass" in the bottle) and Myśliwska (juniper-flavored).

ENTERTAINMENT

Nightlife in Warsaw and Kraków is very cosmopolitan, with a full range of cultural offerings, including theater, opera, ballet, and classical music. In other cities, there is lesser variety,

Religious icons are popular keepsakes that are found in abundance in the Cloth Hall market stalls.

though both Gdańsk and Poznań have healthy schedules of fine arts. Tickets for performances are much more accessibly priced than in most parts of Western Europe and as well in North America.

On the pop culture front, you'll find jazz combos and films from around the world. Big-name international pop and rock bands make only occasional appearances in Poland. You'll find a full roster of bars, pubs, cafés, and nightclubs in the cities, as well as a handful of casinos.

Performing Arts. In the principal cities, Poles are stalwart supporters of the performing arts. In Warsaw, Teatr Wielki (Grand Theater and National Opera; Pl. Teatralny 1; Tel. 692 02 00; <www.teatrwielki.pl>) is the foremost venue in Poland for opera and ballet; Kiri Te Kanawa, Kathleen Battle, and José Carreras have all sung here. For classical music concerts, the National Philharmonic Hall (ul. Jasna 5; Tel. 826 72 81) and the intimate Opera Kameralna (Al. Solidarności 76; Tel. 625 75 10) are among the nation's best. There are also occasional concerts at the Royal Castle on Pl. Zamkowy (Tel. 657 21 70). In Kraków, Słowacki Theater (Pl. Św. Ducha 1; Tel. 423 17 00) is the venue for opera, as well as theater and concerts; for theater and

Amber jewelry is abundant in Gdańsk, but before buying, beware of fakes!

dance, Operetta Stage (ul. Lubicz 48; Tel. 421 16 30); and for music events, the recently renovated Philharmonic Hall (ul. Zwierzyniecka 1; Tel. 422 43 12). Concerts are also held at St. Mary's Cathedral, St. Peter & Paul Church on Wawel Hill and in summer at the Chopin Monument in Łazienki Park. In Gdańsk, the State Baltic Opera (Al. Zwycięstwa 15; Tel. 341 05 63; www.operabaltycka.pl) is one of the best in Poland, and it holds opera and symphonic concerts, while chamber music concerts are held at the Baltic Philharmonic Hall (Ołowianka 1; Tel. 305 20 40). Just outside Gdańsk, in Sopot, the Opera Leśna is an open-air theater for classical and popular music. In Poznań, opera is performed at the Teatr Wielki (ul. Aleksandra Fredry 9; Tel. 852 82 91) and classical music at Filharmonia Poznańska (ul. Św. Marcina 81; Tel. 852 47 08). Poznań is also well known for its acclaimed, long-running ballet company, The Polish Dance Theater-Poznań Ballet (ul. Kozia 4; Tel. 852 42 41).

Dramatic plays are staged almost entirely in Polish, tending to exclude most foreign tourists. Acting and directing are of a very high standard, though, and adventurous theatergoers who don't mind not understanding the language in order to see first-rate acting and production will find plenty of excellent performances, especially in Kraków, the epicenter of the Polish theater world. The Stary Teatr, or Old Theater (ul. Jagiellońska 1; Tel. 422 40 40) is the top venue, with a main stage and two ancillary stages. In Warsaw, top musicals of the Andrew Lloyd Weber variety land at Roma (ul. Konopnickiej 6); the Narodowy, or National Theater (Pl. Teatralny 1) that was recently renovated from head to toe after a devastating fire.

For schedules of opera and classical music concerts, see the local editions of the English-language publication *In Your Pocket,* which contain good round-ups of bars, pubs, and clubs in Warsaw, Kraków, and Gdańsk, as well as *Warsaw Insider,* a free monthly publication in Warsaw.

Larger hotels will also make bookings for you, or you can simply go direct to the venue box office.

Casinos. Casinos Poland runs gaming facilities in hotels in three cities covered in this guide: in Warsaw, Hotel Marriott (Al. Jerozolimskie 65/79; Tel. 630 63 06); in Kraków, Hotel Continental (Novotel) (Al. Armii Krajowej 11; Tel. 637 50 44); and in Poznań, Hotel Merkury (ul. Roosevelt 20; Tel. 855 80 00). In Warsaw, there are also casinos at the Dom Chłopa Hotel (Powstanców Warszawy 2; Tel. 827 58 10); Polonia Hotel (Al. Jerozolimskie 45; Tel. 622 31 23); and Victoria Hotel (ul. Królewska 11; Tel. 827 66 33).

A free bathroom or coat check is a rarity in Poland. In virtually every place — museums, restaurants, etc. — bathrooms carry an obligatory extra charge of 1-2 zł, not just a tip for the attendant.

Cinema. Poland has an enviable cinematic tradition and has produced great film directors who've gone on to international success, including Krzysztof Kieślowski, Andrzej Wajda, and Roman Polański. Poles are dedicated moviegoers, so in the cities you'll find plenty of subtitled Western films on the marquees competing with home-grown product, showing at good, Dolby sound-equipped theaters. Film admissions are cheap by comparison with many countries. Look for the Warsaw Film Festival in October every year.

Clubs and Bars. Poland's towns and cities teem with bars, pubs, cafés, and nightclubs, and Poles have—fairly or unfairly—a reputation as heavy drinkers. The days of hard-drinking men emptying bottles of vodka in plain, poorly lit bars are largely a thing of the past, though, and most young Poles today drink more beer *(piwo)* than vodka and other

Baskets are among the many rustic items on offer at Kraków's Main Market Square.

spirits. You'll find Russian cafés, Irish and English pubs, and discos across Poland.

Bars in atmospheric cellars, and others above ground, have proliferated in recent years in Kraków's Old Town. With so many students in town, they're usually packed. There are so many it is difficult to single out only a few, but among the most interesting are: Black Gallery (ul. Mikołajska 24); Free Pub (ul. Sławkowska 4); Stalowe Magnolie (ul. Św. Jana 15), which has live music and boudoir-style backrooms; U Louisa (Rynek Główny 13);

Bastylia (ul. Stolarska 3); and Alchemia (ul. Estery 5) and Singer Café (ul. Estery 22), in Kazimierz. The distinction between cafés and bars is sometimes difficult to ascertain, but some of the many excellent cafés in Kraków include: Camelot (ul. Św. Tomasza 17), Dym (ul. Św. Tomasza 13), Jama Michalika (ul. Floriańska 45), and Wiśniowy Sad (ul. Grodzka 33). For jazz and blues clubs in Kraków, try U Muniaka (ul. Floriańska 3), Klub Indigo (ul. Floriańska 26), and Klinika 35 (ul. Św. Tomasza 35). Kraków's Old Town also features at least two dozen discos.

Warsaw doesn't have quite as appealing a cluster of bars in one pub-crawl-ready area, but the capital certainly has its share of watering holes and cafés. It has a mini collection of Irish pubs, including Morgan's (ul. Tamka, downstairs from the Chopin Museum), Irish Pub (ul. Miodowa 3), and Cork Irish Pub (Al. Niepodległości 19). Other bars are Lolek (ul. Rokitnicka 20), the elegant Column Bar in the Hotel Bristol (ul. Krakowskie Przedmieście), and John Bull Pub (ul. Jezuicka 4). Nightclubs include Ground Zero (ul. Wspólna 62), Quo Vadis (Pl. Defilad 1), and for jazz & blues Jazz Café Helicon (ul. Freta 45) and Jazz Bistro (ul. Piękna 20).

Gdańsk has a lively roster of pubs in its Main Town. The coolest are Latający Holender (ul. Wały Jagiellońskie 2-4) and Vinifera (ul. Wodopój 7) for wines by the glass. For live jazz, check out Cotton Club (ul. Złotników 25) and Jazz Club (Długi Targ 39).

SPORTS

Poland is, like most European nations, primarily focused on football (soccer), but beyond that sports fever doesn't appear to reach the variety or depth of sports found in many other countries. Poland hasn't yet developed much as a sport-specific destination. That said, the countryside is ideal for out-

At Kraków's Singer Café, many of the tables are made from old Singer sewing machines.

door enthusiasts, and even though most of those destinations are beyond the scope of this guide, visitors interested in horseback-riding, skiing, fishing, and especially hiking have plenty of options.

Golf. If you've just got to play golf on your business trip to Warsaw, head for the First Warsaw Golf and Country Club (Rajszew 70; Tel. 782 45 55; <golfclub@it.com.pl>), an 18-hole course about 30 km (19 miles) outside of the capital. Perhaps the best golfing is near the Baltic Sea, at the Gdańsk Golf and Country Club in Postołów (Tel. 682 83 71).

Hiking and Walking. The vast countryside of Poland is ideal for leisurely walking and more athletic hiking. One of the best areas for both, and especially for serious hikers, are the High Tatra mountains around Zakopane.

Horseback-riding. Equestrian holidays are increasingly popular in Poland; ask your travel agent about Orbis horseback-riding vacations. If you just want to get in the saddle a time or two, contact: Pa-ta-Taj Horse-Riding School (Szkoła Jazdy Konnej) (ul. Krótka 9, Tel. 758 58 35) or Sport and Recreation (Limanki, 26 Luze, Tel. 792 08 42) in Warsaw. There are a couple of dozen stables and riding schools in the environs of the capital; ask for additional information from Tourist Information Centers or your hotel.

Skiing. The hotspot for skiing is Zakopane, at the foot of the High Tatra mountains in southeastern Poland. Skiing is excellent, inexpensive and very popular with Poles and some foreign vacationers on ski packages, even though facilities lag behind resorts in the Alps and Pyrenees.

A klezmer band heats things up at a Kazimierz night spot in Kraków.

Swimming and Water Sports. In Warsaw, the Victoria, Marriott, and Bristol hotels have pools. Less ritzy are these pools: Spartańska (ul. Spartańska 1, Tel. 848 67 46), OSIR (ul. Kasprzaka 1, Tel. 631 48 67), and Merlini's Water Park (ul. Merliniego, Tel. 854 01 30). Kraków also has several pools open to visitors: Wodny Water Park (ul. Dobrego Pasterza 126, Tel. 413 73 99), Sofitel Hotel (ul. M. Konopnickiej 28, Tel. 261 92 12), and Korona (ul. Kalwaryjska 9, Tel. 656 13 68).

The vast majority of boating and other water sports is concentrated in the Mazurian Lakes district in northeastern Poland and the towns along the Bay of Gdańsk, on the Baltic Sea.

Spectator Sports

Football (soccer). Football is Poland's most popular spectator sport. Warsaw's two first-division football teams are Legia Warszawa (ul. Łazienkowska 3, Tel. 628 43 03) and Polonia Warszawa (ul. Konwiktors,a 6, Tel. 635 14 01).

CHILDREN'S POLAND

Poland is not an obvious place to take children, perhaps, and in fact few foreigners who haven't been posted overseas in Poland seem to do it. Traveling with children in Poland is a matter of being flexible, creative, and putting together disparate activities to keep the kids interested when palaces, castles, and rebuilt old towns impress them less than they do their parents. Many of the activities listed below are in the capital, Warsaw, where there is simply a greater abundance of facilities.

To begin with the most obvious option, the Warsaw Zoo (ul. Ratuszowa 1-3, Tel. 619 40 41, <www.warszawa.um .gov.pl./zoo>) has been going strong since 1928. The habitats of some 4000 animals, including Siberian tigers, kangaroos,

cheetahs, crocs, snow leopards, and an unusual red panda are spread across 40 hectares (99 acres). The zoo also has a free-flight bird hall. Another option in the capital for small children is the Baj Puppet Theater (ul. Jagiellońska 28, Tel. 818 08 21) housed in a former Jewish school in Praga, across the river from Old Town. Playgrounds — the kind with tunnels, jungle gyms, and inflatable cages filled with rubber balls — are found in the capital: Stratosfera (ul. Ostrobramska 75c, Tel. 611 35 83); Kolorado Ursynów (ul. Herbsta 4, Tel. 664 88 77).

For kids with energy to burn, there are water parks and swimming pools (see above) in summer and ice rinks in winter. To go ice skating, check out the Stegny Skating Track (Tor Łyżwiarski Stegny), (ul. Inspektowa 1, Tel. 842 27 68) or Torwar (ul. Łazienkowska, Tel. 621 44 71) in Warsaw. Another activity that is all the rage is paintball, and there

> As in most European countries, the numbers of floors in buildings don't begin with the lobby but the first flight up.

are multiple fields where you can inflict paint rather than pain. Try Marcus-Graf (ul. Widok 10, in Beniaminów near Warsaw; Tel. 816 10 08), TM Pretor (ul. Zaaruskiego 6, Warsaw; Tel. 838 25 35), Rival Paintball Guns (ul. Bartosika 10/77, Warsaw; Tel. 671 22 63), or Extreme Sports (ul. Klaudyny 18/5, Warsaw; Tel. 833 73 73). Paintballers in Kraków should check out Ultimate Sports (near fort Bodzanów; Tel. 431 20 61).

Another fast-paced sport is go-karts. In Warsaw, race the kids over to Imola, where they also feature paintball (ul. Puławska 33, Piaseczno; Tel. 648 27 14). If your kids like

Zakopane is a hot spot in cold weather, offering winter sports enthusiasts excellent skiing at reasonable rates.

Children love watching other children compete and in Poland, soccer is THE game to watch on playgrounds and in parks.

bowling, you'll find facilities in all the major cities. One place they're sure to like in Kraków is Atomic World Entertainment Center (ul. Zakopiańska 62; Tel. 261 31 14), which not only has swanky lanes but loads of video games, billiards, and air hockey. In the Malta lake district of Poznań, there are many facilities ideal for children, including a manmade ski slope and a exhilerating toboggan run.

For older kids that enjoy hiking and skiing, the area around Zakopane in the Tatra mountains is the best in Poland. Among traditional sights, two stand out as especially appealing, or educational, for children. The 700-year-old Wieliczka Salt Mine (near Kraków) — where you first descend 378 steps, then traipse through long corridors and see chapels and figures (including the Seven Dwarves) entirely carved out of salt, and finally zoom up to ground level via a fast and slightly shaky bare-bones elevator — is sure to be cool for kids. Also near Kraków is one visit older children are sure not to forget, though it may demand a lot of explaining and soul-searching on your and their parts. A visit to the Auschwitz concentration camp may not exactly be "fun," but it certainly is a tremendous and moving learning experience for older children. The administrators of Auschwitz in fact recommend that children under the age of 13 not visit the camp, because the horrors of what happened there, to adults and children, are all too graphic and disturbing.

HELPFUL EXPRESSIONS

wejście	entrance	**ulica (ul.)**	street
wyjście	exit	**plac (Pl.)**	square
otwarte	open	**aleja (Al.)**	avenue
zamknięte	closed	**skwer**	boulevard
ciągnąć	pull	**rynek**	market square
pchać	push	**centrum**	city center
		informacja	information

Tax Refunds

In Poland, Value Added Tax (VAT) is included in the sales price listed. Foreigners are eligible to reclaim the Polish national sales tax of up to 16.5 percent on single-store purchases (except on art and antiques purchases). The minimum purchase at Global Refund affiliated stores is 200 zł. Look for the blue-and-white signs, posted in participating shops, that read "Tax Free for Tourists." At the time of departure from Poland, cash and credit card refunds can be made at airports, as well as the Stena Line Ferry in Gdynia. Visitors must present the purchase along with the refund claim and original invoice (in the Tax Free envelope) to the customs officer upon departure. These forms are acquired at the participating store where the purchase is made. For additional information on obtaining refunds, contact Global Refund Poland (Tel. 48 22/853 37 55 or 800/KNOW-VAT; <www.globalrefund.com>).

CALENDAR OF EVENTS

February International Festival of Sailors' Songs (Shanties), Warsaw

April Festival of Contemporary Music, Poznań

March/April Holy Week religious celebrations, all Poland

March Poznań Jazz Festival, Poznań

April/May Warsaw Ballet Days, Warsaw

May Music and Art Festival, Toruń

International Book Fair, Warsaw

Jazz Festival, Poznań

June International Theater Festival, Poznań

Summer Jazz Days, Warsaw

Jewish Culture Festival, Kraków

24 June St. John's Feast Day, especially in Warsaw, Kraków and Poznań

June/July Mozart Festival, Warsaw

Theater Summer Festival, Zamość

July Summer Festival of Early Music, Kraków

Summer Festival of Opera, Kraków

August International Song Festival, Sopot

International Festival of Old Music, Kraków

International Festival of Highland Folklore, Zakopane

September International Violin Makers Competition, Poznań

October Chopin International Piano Competition (every 5 years; next in 2005)

Warsaw Film Festival, Warsaw

International Jazz Festival, Warsaw

November 1 All Saints Day

All Saints Day Jazz Festival, Kraków

Warsaw Ancient Music Festival, Warsaw

December Most Beautiful Nativity Scene Contest, Kraków

EATING OUT

Polish cuisine is rich, heavy, simple, high in calories, and served in large portions. Sauces tend to be fatty and thick, potatoes and dumplings are a staple, and vegetables are not a standard accompaniment—they almost always cost extra. Spices are few: salt, pepper, dill. Given its shifting borders over the centuries, it's not surprising that Polish cooking counts on the influence of several national cuisines, namely Ukrainian, German, Lithuanian, and Russian.

People in other countries are frequently familiar with certain items common in the Polish diet, including *pierogi* (stuffed dumplings), *barszcz* (beet root soup), and *żywiecka* (Polish sausage), as well as the ubiquitous menu items borsch and sauerkraut. Probably the most traditional Polish dish is *bigos* ("hunter's stew"), a sauerkraut dish laced with several meats (pork, game, sausage, bacon and more).

> On menus at restaurants, main courses do not usually include accompaniments. Potatoes, salads, and other items are listed under *dodatki* and served at additional cost.

The restaurant scene in Poland, like most everything else, has changed dramatically in the years since the fall of the Communist regime. Eating out, at least as far as fine dining was concerned, used to be a rarity, and shortages and rationing were common. No longer. Restaurants of all stripes have blossomed in major towns, though traditional restaurants serving classic Polish cuisine have not disappeared, thankfully. They should be the focus of any visitor's dining habits in Poland.

Where to Eat

Most visitors will eat the majority of their meals in a *restauracja* (restaurant), which has table service. These

*Partake in the simple pleasure of rustic Polish cuisine —
healthy, hearty, and heavy on the beets.*

range from inexpensive eateries where office workers take
their lunch to upscale dining rooms frequented far more by
foreign visitors and a small handful of elite Poles than by
common citizens.

A café *(kawiarnia)* is not strictly a coffeehouse. Most
also have a menu and serve everything from snacks to full

meals at all hours of the day. Another eatery is the cheap, cafeteria-style, self-service creature called a *bar mleczny,* literally a milk bar. Often you can get a good, home-cooked and filling plate for very little.

When to Eat

Breakfast *(śniadanie)* is generally served between 7 and 10am. Poles may eat bread or a croissant served with butter, cheese, and ham or sausage. Eggs for breakfast are not uncommon. At most upscale hotels, a basic international breakfast buffet is generally served. Often you will find local pastries and possibly some foods you may not think of as usual breakfast fare, such as stuffed cabbage and other more hearty regional specialties.

Lunch *(obiad),* generally served between 2 and 4pm or even later, is the main meal of the day for Poles, a fact reflected in the quantities that tend to be served at midday. The obiad is typically soup, main course, and dessert.

Dinner *(kolacja)* is served mid-evening, and it can be similar and nearly as substantial as the obiad or considerably lighter, more a mirror of breakfast.

Polish Cooking

Certain ingredients are essential to traditional Polish cuisine: sauerkraut, vegetables, fruits, and mushrooms. One of the most distinctive flavors of Polish cooking is sourness, but it can also be hot or sweet.

Most food is cooked in lard rather than oil or butter (some restaurants cook only in goose fat). This tends to give it a heavier, richer taste than many Westerners are accustomed to. If portions are too hefty for you, order soup and then an appetizer instead of the main course.

Soups *(zupa).* Soups are immensely popular with locals and always on the menu. Most Poles think a meal incomplete without soup (some visitors may find Polish soups, on the other hand, to be complete meals). *Barszcz czerwony* (red beetroot soup with carrots, celery and leek) is an ancient recipe; the authentic version has a sour taste. It can be served clear or with cream and with small ravioli-like dumplings. Beet root soup made with vegetable stock and served with mushroom-filled *uszka* (thin ravioli) is traditional for Christmas Eve. Żurek, or white *barszcz,* is made from rye flour and fermented with spices. It is sometimes served with sausage or a hardboiled egg. *Chłodnik* is a cold beetroot summer soup with sour milk and thick cream, combined with beets, cucumbers, radishes, chives, dill and other vegetables. Sometimes crab or veal is added. *Ogórkowa* (dill cucumber soup) is also sour, as is *kapuśniak* (sauerkraut soup with potatoes). Other soups to enjoy are *grzybowa* (mushroom soup) and *szczawiowa,* or sorrel soup.

In public bathrooms, the men's room is often indicated by a triangle; the women's by a circle.	
toilets	toalety
men	panowie (męski)
women	panie (damski)

Starters *(przekąski).* The classic starter is herring, often served with sauces like oil, vinegar, or mayonnaise, and lots of onions. Steak tartare *(befsztyk tatarski)* — raw minced beef with egg yolk, chopped onions, spices, olive oil, salt, and lemon juice — is a favorite of Poles. You'll also find jellied carp, pike, and smoked eel for appetizers, and something few foreigners try: pig's foot or knuckles in aspic. (Try it with a shot of vodka.)

Traditional Polish Dishes. The pierogi is the undisputed Polish folk dish, originally from Russia and dating back to medieval times. They can be sweet or savory. Ravioli-like dumplings are filled with a variety of stuffings, including fresh or sour cabbage, mushrooms (and cabbage), cheese, and potatoes, and fruits like apples and blackberries. Small pierogi often are served in soups. Stuffed cabbage is another traditional dish, with leaves filled with meat, meat and barley, buck wheat, or cheese, usually covered with cream or tomato sauce. Poles are also very fond of potato pancakes and potato dumplings.

Outdoor eating at Café Ariel, the longstanding Jewish (non-kosher) restaurant in Kazimierz.

Meat *(mięso; dania mięsne).* Poland is a nation of avid carnivores, and to most Poles, a meal of substance includes meat. Pork is by far the most popular meat dish. The classic preparation is a pork cutlet prepared with fried onions, coated in bread crumbs or toast and served with stewed cabbage. Pork roast is eaten both hot and cold. Hot pot roast may be served with dried prunes and doused with red wine. Beef is less common, though *zrazy zawijane* (beef rolls filled with bacon, dark bread, sour cucumbers and

Zakopane is known for its distinctive artisinal cheeses. Don't even try to resist them!

mushrooms) is a standard dish. *Flaki po polsku* (tripe stew) is thin strips of beef tripe, boiled in meat and vegetable stock and served with dark bread. The meat dish not to be missed in Poland is *bigos,* a classic hunter's preparation. It is fresh and sour cabbage, often stewed for several days with a number of different types of meat and sausage (meat and cabbage in equal proportion). It is the supreme winter meal in Poland.

Game *(dziczyzna)* and fowl *(drób)*. Game is very popular, as you might expect from the national affinity for meat and rich tastes. Venison *(sarna)* is usually reserved for elite restaurants, as are wild boar *(dzik)* and other "exotic" game. Look, too, for hare *(zając)* and pheasant *(bażant)*. Chicken *(kurczak)* is popular and not expensive. Polish chicken is stuffed with liver, rye bread, egg, spices and parsley, and roasted. Roasted duck *(kaczka)* with apples is another favorite.

Fish *(dania rybne)*. Fish is decidedly less common on menus than pork and other meats, but pike, eel, perch, sturgeon and others — boiled, fried or roasted — are found in most good restaurants. Carp is a particular favorite (especially on Christmas Eve), often served in aspic or Polish sauce with raisins and almonds.

The National Spirit

Vodka, the national spirit, is heavily ritualized. When you visit someone in his or her house, it's polite to take a bottle — yes, a bottle — which is expected to be emptied before the evening is over. Poles drink vodka neat — in one gulp, like tequila — never sipped, and usually not in cocktails (though a Tatanka, Żubrówka vodka mixed with apple juice, is popular with young people).

Vegetables *(potrawy jarskie).* Vegetarian restaurants are still a rarity in Poland, though classic milk bars began basically as vegetarian places, most having now added a few meat dishes. Vegetable accompaniments usually have to be ordered separately and can be uninspired. Vegetarians should steer toward dumplings stuffed with fruit, *kopytka* (gnoccis), pierogi filled with cottage cheese, and crepes. Salads include tomato salads, cucumbers in sour cream, and sauerkraut.

Desserts *(desery).* Poles are great eaters of pastries and sweets. Among those you're likely to find on menus and fellow diners' plates are cream puffs, *eklerka* (éclairs), *napoleonki* (millefeuille), *sernik* (cheesecake), apple tarts, and traditional *mazurki* — thin flat cakes topped with nuts and fruits.

Drinks

Poland doesn't produce wine. Imported wines are available in nicer restaurants; the cheaper varieties are Hungarian and Bulgarian. You'll also find French, Italian, and Spanish wines, but pay for the privilege.

Poles and Russians may bicker about who created it, but vodka *(wódka)* is a staple of the Polish diet. It is mostly clear, though you'll also find slightly brown and flavored versions. Wyborowa is the standard-bearer; look also for Żubrówka (which is flavored with a strand of bison grass from the

smacznego	bon appétit
Na zdrowie!	Cheers!
Proszę o rachunek.	Check, please.

Białowieża forest), *żytnia* (rye vodka), *Goldwasser* (from Gdańsk, thick and sweet and spiked with 23-carat gold flecks), *myśliwska* (flavored with juniper berries) and kosher vodkas.

Polish beers, or *piwo* (such as Żywiec and Okocim) go well with heavy, spicy foods; except at the most formal of restaurants, it is as acceptable to drink beer with a meal as it is wine. Polish beers, generally served in pint glasses, are generally light and drinkable, although they cannot be compared with their Czech, German, Belgian, or English counterparts.

Coffee *(kawa)* is a favorite drink of Poles and is often served Turkish style, strong with a dash of milk. Espresso and capuccino are now quite common. Tea *(herbata),* usually served with lemon, is drunk by most Poles.

International soft drinks and mineral water *(woda mineralna)* are readily available.

Menu Reader

mięso	meat	**chleb**	bread
ryba	fish	**ser**	cheese
zupa	soup	**szynka**	ham
żurek	rye-flour soup	**frytki**	fries/chips
befsztyk	beef steak	**ziemniaki**	potatoes
bigos	sauerkraut and meat dish	**ryż**	rice
		sałatka	salad
golonka	boiled pig's knuckle	**barszcz**	beetroot soup
		flaki	tripe
gołąbki	stuffed cabbage leaves	**grzybowa**	mushroom
		jarzynowa	vegetable
kotlet	fried pork cutlet	**ogórkowa**	cucumber
polędwica	beef	**lody**	ice cream
zrazy	stuffed beef rolls	**herbata**	tea
		kawa	coffee
kurczak	chicken	**wódka**	vodka
kaczka	duck	**woda**	water
pierogi	dumplings	**piwo**	beer
pstrąg	trout		

HANDY TRAVEL TIPS

An A–Z Summary of Practical Information

A

ACCOMMODATIONS (*hotel/pokój*) (See also CAMPING, YOUTH HOSTELS, and RECOMMENDED HOTELS)

Hotels in Poland are unofficially graded from one star to five stars, and those rating three to five are of comparable international standard. In many cities, there is a shortage of good hotels; there is especially a dearth of good three-star hotels and few, if any, two- or one-star hotels that can be recommended. Warsaw and Kraków have a large number of top-flight, five-star hotels targeting business travelers and upscale tourists. The Orbis chain used to have a virtual monopoly on mid- and top-level hotels; such is no longer the case, as international chains and independents have increased the competition.

If all the higher grade hotels are full, or beyond your budget, the best option is to stay slightly out of town in a pension or bed-and-breakfast hotel. Other options to consider are accommodations in private homes or a self-catering apartment. Accommodations in private homes (kwatery prywatne) are common throughout Poland. There are also more than 200 registered campsites and a network of youth hostels in the major cities.

It is essential to book ahead during peak season (May to October). Tourism Information Offices (including the one at the airport) will provide lists of accommodations.

Room prices, which should be posted at the reception desk, usually include VAT (value-added tax) and often but not always include breakfast. Outside of the most expensive hotels, in general prices lag behind those of other European countries. Confusingly, hotels may list their prices in US dollars, German marks, euros, or Polish złoty.

Do you have a room?	**Czy są wolne pokoje?**
How much is it?	**Ile kosztuje?**
single	**pojedynczy pokój**
double	**podwójny pokój**

Poland

without bath	**bez łazienki**
with bath	**z łazienką**
expensive	**drogi**

AIRPORTS *(lotnisko)*

Warsaw: International flights arrive and depart from Okęcie International Airport, south of the capital. There are rental car agencies, left luggage, money exchange desks, ATM machines, and an information office.

It takes about 30 minutes to get from the airport to the center of Warsaw. A taxi will cost upwards of 20 zł (30 zł at night). The taxis waiting out front, though they look official, are almost all "mafia taxis," and will cheat you as much as they can. If you must take a taxi, call for one at the information desk: Radio Taxi (Tel. 919), Super Taxi (Tel. 9622), or Express Taxi (Tel. 9626). By bus (5am to 10:30pm), take no. 175 to the city center (watch out for pickpockets); the bus stops at all red bus stops and Centralna train station. The faster yellow "Airport City" bus line goes to Warszawa Centralna and major hotels (6am-11pm); the limousine service "Fly & Drive" (Tel. 22/650-3030) will take you directly to your hotel. Airport Information: Tel. 22/650 41 00.

Kraków: Balice Airport, also known as John Paul II International Airport, is 18 km west of town. To town, take a taxi (call Euro Taxi, Tel. 9664; Metro Taxi, Tel. 9667; or Radio Taxi, Tel. 919; 40-60 zł) or bus no. 152, which goes to the Old Town and train station. Airport information: Tel. 12/411 19 55.

Gdańsk: Flights from London and a handful of other European cities (Hamburg, Copenhagen, Brussels) land at Port Lotniczy Gdańsk Trójmiasto, west of the city center. A taxi will cost between 30-40 zł; call a taxi (Eskort Radio Taxi, Tel. 9624; Hallo, Tel. 9197) for pickup rather than taking a waiting mafia cab . Bus B from the airport to the main train station in Gdańsk (40 minutes). Airport information: Tel. 58/348 11 54.

B

BUDGETING FOR YOUR TRIP

Though prices have risen dramatically in the past few years, Poland remains inexpensive for most visitors from Western Europe and North America relative to other European capital cities. Still, visitors expecting the dirt-cheap Central Europe of the very recent past may be in for a bit of a surprise. Four- and five-star hotels in Warsaw and Kraków are now nearly as costly as those in Western Europe. Many facets of daily life remain true bargains for visitors: the highly efficient public transport system, restaurants and cafés, and museums and concert performances.

Transportation to Poland. For most Europeans, Warsaw or Kraków is a short, fairly inexpensive flight or train ride away. North Americans (and of course Australians, New Zealanders, and South Africans) can expect their flights to eat up considerably more of their budgets—anywhere from $700 to $1000 or more, though off-season roundtrip deals on Polish LOT from New York and Canada can sometimes be had for as little as $500.

Accommodations. Confusingly, hotels may list their prices in US dollars, German marks, euros or Polish złoty. Hotels at the top levels are close if not equal to what you might expect to find in other European capitals. Double room in high season, central Warsaw or Kraków: 5-star hotel 400-1,000 zł ($100-250); 3- to 4-star hotel 150-400 zł ($40-100); 2-star hotel or pension 40-150 zł ($10-40).

Meals and Drinks. Dining out in Poland remains a bargain except at the most upscale and famous restaurants. A three-course meal for two, with wine and service, in a moderate restaurant should run 80 zł ($20); at an expensive restaurant, 160 zł ($40) or more.

Local Transportation. Public transportation is inexpensive whether bus, tram, or Metro (subway) (2-4 zł). Only taxis are relatively expensive

Poland

(and especially if you wind up in an unofficial "mafia" taxi). Opt for public transportation except in rare instances (after-hours), and always call for a taxi rather than hail one on the street.

Incidentals. Car rental is expensive: Daily rates in U.S. $, including unlimited mileage, range from $70-$100/day for an economy-size car, including CDW insurance. At press time, gasoline cost 3.50 zł per liter. Museum admission: 4 zł. Entertainment: Theater, musicals, and classical music concerts generally range from 20 zł.

C

CAR RENTAL (See also DRIVING)
Renting a car in Poland isn't a great idea unless you intend to explore the countryside in considerable depth. Car rentals are expensive ($70-$100/day), and the road network in Poland leaves much to be desired; roads are in need of repair and only one highway to speak of exists (and it isn't between Warsaw and Kraków). Arrangements and conditions for car rental are similar to those in other countries. The minimum age requirement is 21 and you must have been in possession of a valid license for at least one year. U.S. and Canadian licenses are accepted as are international driving licenses.

Ask if CDW insurance is included in the price. There are a few local agencies, such as GlobalPoland (Warsaw, Tel. 846 03 02), which tend to be cheaper, in addition to the major international agencies, including Avis (Warsaw, Al. Jerozolimskie 65-Marriott Hotel, Tel. 630 73 16; Kraków, ul. Basztowa 15, Tel. 421 10 66), Budget (Warsaw, Al. Jerozolimskie 65-Marriott Hotel, Tel. 630 72 80), Europcar (Warsaw, airport, Tel. 650 25 64; Kraków, ul. Krowoderska 58, Tel. 633 77 73), Hertz (Warsaw, ul. Nowogrodzka 27, Tel. 621 02 39; Kraków, Al. Focha 1, Tel. 429 62 62), and National (Warsaw, Airport, Tel. 606 92 42; Kraków, ul. Głowackiego 22, Tel. 636 86 30).

gas (petrol) station   **stacja benzynowa**

CLIMATE

All of Poland is very cold in winter and warm but comfortable in summer. The best weather (and time to visit) is from May to early June and September-October. Temperatures in the highlands around Zakopane are very cold in winter.

The chart below shows the average daytime temperature for Warsaw:

°F	J	F	M	A	M	J	J	A	S	O	N	D
°C	-1	-2	3	12	15	18	17	18	12	12	6	1

CLOTHING

Poles in the big cities—especially Warsaw, Kraków and Gdynia—are style-conscious, and chic Western fashions are very much in evidence. A jacket and tie would only be suggested at special theater or opera occasions or very exclusive restaurants. Attire in the countryside is very informal.

CRIME AND SAFETY (See also EMERGENCIES and POLICE)

Crime has risen considerably in Polish cities (13% in 2000), and Warsaw cannot be considered a safe place. As far as visitors are concerned, the major crime is pickpocketing (usually on buses and trams) or car theft. Take the usual precautions, especially on trips to and from the airport and the train station. Assaults are not unheard of, and drug-related crimes are a particular danger.

Other cities, including Kraków, are generally safer, though always be careful in areas frequented by tourists (Wawel Hill, Market Square). The tri-cities area of Gdańsk, Gdynia, and Sopot has a high incidence of muggings, sometimes in broad daylight.

Organized groups of thieves and pickpockets sometimes operate at major tourist destinations, in train stations, and on trains, trams, and buses in major cities. Thefts have occurred on overnight trains, especially in second-class closed compartments, though the most common occurrence is when boarding. Car thefts, car-jackings, and theft from cars are commonplace. If driving, do not pull over if another driver intimates that something is wrong with your car; it is very likely a set-up for a robbery. There are also reports of thieves opening or breaking passenger-side doors and windows in slow or stopped traffic.

CUSTOMS AND ENTRY REQUIREMENTS (See also EMBASSIES AND CONSULATES)

All visitors require a valid passport to enter Poland. The citizens of many countries, including most European nations and the US, do not need a visa. However, citizens of Australia, New Zealand, Canada and South Africa require visas. Visas, good for 90 days, can be obtained from any Polish diplomatic mission; this usually takes 24 hours.

For customs questions, call Tel. 22/811 01 28.

Currency restrictions. There is no limit on the amount of foreign currency that can be brought into Poland, though excessive amounts should be declared at customs upon arrival.

The export of works of art created before 1945 is prohibited; works of art produced by living artists after 1945 may be exported with permission from the National Museum/Provincial Conservator of Relics (so too can some pre-1945 works if the National Museum judges them not to be "of museum quality"). Certain works of art produced after 1945 may still be subject to a ban on exportation if the artist is no longer living and the work is deemed of high cultural value. Those desiring to export a pre-1945 art work must get a document certifying such by the National Museum Department of Art Certification (Dział Opiniowania Dzieł Sztuki), ul. Myśliwiecka 1, Warsaw.

D

DRIVING (See also CAR RENTAL)

To take your car into Poland you need a valid driving license and automobile registration papers. Cars from most European countries (including Britain, Germany, and Austria) are presumed to be fully insured, so no extra documentation need be shown. To be safe, carry proof of insurance.

Road Conditions. Poland is not a great place to drive your own vehicle. It is reputed to have the highest accident mortality rates in Europe, and roads are in generally poor condition (one publication estimates the roads in Warsaw to be 45% in disrepair). There is no system of highways crisscrossing the country (there is just one "superhighway," from Kraków to Katowice), so traveling by car can be slow-going, since cars often have to compete with trucks and every other vehicle on the road. This is what the US State Department has to say about driving in Poland: "Driving, especially after dark, is very hazardous. Roads are generally narrow, badly lit, and frequently under repair, especially in the summer months. Roads are often used by pedestrians and animals as well as by vehicles. Heavy alcohol consumption is frequently a contributing factor in accidents."

Rules and Regulations. Drive on the right and pass on the left, but be careful at all times. Cars must be fitted with a nationality plate or sticker. A set of spare bulbs, a first-aid kit, and a warning triangle are also obligatory. Seat belts are compulsory in front and back seats; children under 12 are prohibited from traveling in the front seat. Motorcycle riders and passengers must wear crash helmets. Using a cellular phone while driving is prohibited. Drinking and driving laws are tough; an amount of alcohol in the bloodstream above 0.02% is a punishable violation.

Speed limits are 130 km/h (80 mph) on highways, 110 km/h (69 mph) on expressways, 90 km/h (55 mph) outside of urban areas, and 60 km/h (37 mph) in built-up areas (but 50 km/h, or 31 mph in Warsaw). You may be fined on the spot for speeding.

Fuel costs *(benzyna)*. Filling stations are common along highways and main roads, but don't venture down minor roads without filling up. Stations are usually open 24 hours. Unleaded fuel is widely available (about 3.50 zł). Only in the rarest of cases are credit cards not accepted for payment.

Parking. Parking is a major problem in any of the big cities, especially where historic centers are pedestrian-only. If you are driving, check that your hotel has parking facilities. A car parked in a prohibited zone will be towed away.

If You Need Help. For roadside assistance SOS, call Tel. 981. Remember to put out the red warning triangle 50m (55 yd) behind your car. If anyone is injured, the police must be notified.

Road Signs. Standard international pictographs are in use all over Poland.

Length

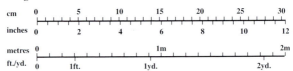

Distance

car	**auto/samochód**
unleaded fuel	**benzyna bezołowiowa**
parking	**parking**
detour	**objazd**
gas/petrol	**benzyna**
gas station	**stacja benzynowa**
repair	**naprawić**
breakdown	**awaria**
no passing	**zakaz wyprzedzania**

E

ELECTRICITY

The current is 220 volts AC, 50 Hertz throughout Poland. Plugs are the standard continental (2-prong) type, for which British and North American appliances need an adapter. Electrical equipment of 110V/60Hz requires an adapter or voltage converter. Short-term power outages are not uncommon.

EMBASSIES AND CONSULATES

Embassies are located in Warsaw; a few nations have consulates in other cities, notably Kraków and Gdańsk.

Australia: Embassy, ul. Nowogrodzka 11; Tel. 521 34 44.

Canada: Embassy, Al. Jerozolimskie 123, 10th floor; Tel. 629 80 51.

Ireland: Consulate (Warsaw), ul. Humańska 10; Tel. 849 66 55.

New Zealand: Embassy, ul. Migdałowa 4; Tel. 645 14 07.

South Africa: Consulate (Warsaw), ul. Koszykowa 54; Tel. 625 62 28.

U.K.: Embassy, Al. Róż 1; Tel. 628 10 01. Consulate (Kraków), ul. Św. Anny 41; Tel. 656 23 36. Consulate (Gdańsk), Al. Grunwaldzka 102; Tel. 341 43 65.

U.S.: Embassy, Al. Ujazdowskie 29/31; Tel. 628 30 41. Consulate (Kraków), ul. Stolarska 9; Tel. 429 66 55.

EMERGENCIES *(pogotowie ratunkowe)* (See also EMBASSIES AND CONSULATES, HEALTH AND MEDICAL CARE, POLICE, and CRIME AND SAFETY)
Emergency telephone numbers (toll-free but generally non-English-speaking) throughout Poland:

General emergency	**999**
Ambulance	**999**

Poland

Fire	**998**
Police	**997**
Roadside Assistance	**981 or 9633**
24-hour medical service	**999 or 9439**

ambulance	**karetka pogotowia**
doctor	**lekarz**
hospital	**szpital**
police	**policja**

G

GAY AND LESBIAN TRAVELERS

As a fervently Catholic and conservative country, gay life is not much out in the open in Poland. Still, there are gay scenes in Warsaw and Kraków and to a lesser extent smaller cities. Two organizations to contact in Warsaw are: Lambda (ul. Czerniakowska 178/16; Tel. 628 52 22; <lambdawa@polbox.com>); and Pride Society (<pridesociety@yahoo.com>). For information on gay Poland, check out the web sites <www.gay.pl> and <www.gejowo.com.pl>. One of the top gay nightclubs in Warsaw is Mykonos (ul. Wałbrzyska 11).

GETTING THERE

Air Travel. The major European airlines service Poland, as do the major American and Canadian carriers. The Polish National carrier, LOT Polish Airlines, flies from most major European cities and from North America. Scheduled flights are also available from British Airways. From the northeast coast of the US, flying time to Warsaw is about 8 hours.

International Airport. Warsaw's Okęcie airport is the primary international airport, though those in Kraków, Gdańsk, Poznań, and others also handle a few international flights. Kraków's Balice International Airport has been refurbished and its capacity for international flights expanded.

Rail Travel. Warsaw and Kraków, among other cities, can easily be reached from any major Western, Central, or Eastern European city. From the UK, trains depart from London's Victoria station, arriving at Warsaw some 30 hours later. The most direct route is via Dover to Ostend and Berlin or Prague.

The following international rail passes are valid in Poland: InterRail, Euro Domino, EurailPass (and its variants), European East Pass, and Polrailpass. In the U.S. Tel. (800) 4 EURAIL.

Warsaw's international railway station is Warszawa Centralna (Tel. 9436). In Kraków, it is Kraków Główny (Tel. 624 54 39).

By Car/Coach. Warsaw is connected by major highway to Berlin, Prague, Budapest, and Vienna. The cheapest way to get from London to Warsaw is by coach, which takes just short of a day and a half. Eurolines (<www.eurolines.com>) and other European bus companies make the trek, as do Polish companies like Pekaes (Tel. 22 621 34 69). and Orbis Transport (Tel. 22 846 22 53). If you plan to drive across the Continent, the most direct route is via Ostend, Brussels, and Berlin. Buses from across Europe arrive at Warszawa Zachodnia (Warsaw West) station (Tel.9433).

GUIDES AND TOURS

A good number of travel agencies and organizations in many countries operate organized sightseeing tours of Poland. A few offer specialized trips, such as Jewish pilgrimage tours and religious-oriented tours to "Sanctuaries of Poland" (Classic Travel, Inc; Tel. 800/774-6996). Other specialty tours include "Schindler's List tours" in Kazimierz, the old Jewish quarter of Kraków.

Orbis is the largest tour operator in Poland and it offers everything from city tours to day trips to best-of-Poland trips, as do most travel agencies. For foreign-language guides and guided tours in major cities, contact the tourism information office or local office of the travel agent PTTK.

H

HEALTH AND MEDICAL CARE (See also EMERGENCIES)

Polish doctors and other health officials are generally knowledgeable and skilled, and most speak some English and German. But the under-funded hospital system is facing strains. However, according to the U.S. State Department, "Adequate medical care is available in Poland, but it generally does not meet Western standards." Doctors and hospitals may expect immediate cash payment for health services. Be sure to check with your insurance company to confirm whether your policy applies overseas, including provision for medical evacuation.

Tap water is potable but many travelers opt for bottled water for matters of taste.

Emergency medical treatment on the scene is available for foreigners. Ask at your hotel desk or consulate for the name of a doctor who speaks your language. In Warsaw, call Falck dispatchers (Tel. 9675) for English-language emergency services. The Central Emergency Medical Center is located at ul. Hoża 56 (corner of ul. Poznańska). A private hospital with a good reputation is Hospital of the Ministry of Internal Affairs (ul. Wołoska 137; Tel. 602 15 78). In Kraków, a general health care information line is Tel. 422 05 11.

For 24-hour medical information, including advice about private clinics, call Tel. 9439.

Pharmacies. Look for the sign *apteka*. In Poland these shops only sell pharmaceutical and related products. Tourism Information Offices have lists of night pharmacies. In Warsaw, two are: Apteka (ul. Puławska 39 Tel. 849 37 57) and Apteka Grabowskiego (Al. Jerozolimskie 5, Centralny Station; Tel. 825 69 86). Local editions of In Your Pocket list additional pharmacies.

Where's the nearest pharmacy?	**Gdzie jest najbliższa apteka?**
I need a doctor/dentist.	**Ja potrzebuję doktora/dentystę.**

HOLIDAYS

1 January	New Year's Day
1 May	Labor Day
3 May	Constitution Day
June	Corpus Christi
15 August	Assumption Day
1 November	All Saints' Day
11 November	National Independence Day
25-26 December	Christmas
Moveable date	(April) Easter

I

INTERNET CAFES

Internet cafés are very popular in Poland's bigger cities, and prices are very inexpensive, from 4-6 zł/hour.

Warsaw:

Studio.tpi (ul. Świętokrzyska 3; Tel. 826 59 53; Mon-Fri, 10am-11pm; Sat-Sun, 12pm-11pm).

Casablanca Café (ul. Krakowskie Przedmieście 4/6; Tel. 828 14 47; daily, 9:30am-1:30am)

Kraków:

Centrum Internet (Rynek Główny 9, Pasaż Bielaka; Tel. 431 21 84; 24 hours.

U Louisa (Rynek Główny 13; 11am-11pm)

L

LANGUAGE

Polish, a Slavic language, is the mother tongue of 99 percent of the population. The most widely known foreign language is German, though English is quickly gaining on it and is far more popular than German among younger people. In cities English speakers are unlikely to encounter many problems, as most people they'll

Poland

encounter speak at least some English (many Poles are extremely
fluent in English and other languages). In the countryside, commu-
nication difficulties are to be expected. Polish is extremely difficult,
but learning even a handful of key phrases is a good idea and will
prove helpful.

Here are a few useful phrases and some signs you are likely to see:

yes	**tak**
no	**nie**
Hi. (informal, singular/plural)	**Cześć.**
How are you?	**Jak sie**
(formal)	**pan**
(informal)	**pani (m/f) miewa?**
Very well, thanks.	**Dziękuję, bardzo dobrze.**
Good night.	**Dobranoc.**
Goodbye.	**Do widzenia.**
Thank you (very much).	**Dziękuję (bardzo).**
Excuse me (sorry).	**Przepraszam.**
Do you speak English?	**Czy Pan/Pani mówi po**
	angielsku?
I don't understand.	**Nie rozumiem.**
I understand.	**Rozumiem.**
I don't know.	**Nie wiem.**
Where is…?	**Gdzie jest…?**
How do I get to…?	**Jak dojechać do…?**
How far is it to…?	**Jak daleko jest do…?**
Good morning/day.	**Dzień dobry. (jen doe-bri)**
Good afternoon.	**Dobry wieczór.**
Good evening.	**Dobry wieczór.**
	(do-bri vee-a ye-chor)
Nice to meet you.	**Bardzo mi miło.**
	(bardzo mee mee-who)
You're welcome.	**Proszę. (pro-sha)**
Please.	**Proszę. (pro-sha)**

Help!	**Pomocy! (po-mo-tsay)**
Hi/bye.	**Cześć. (chesh)**
Where is the toilet?	**Gdzie są toalety?**
May I have…?	**Czy mogę…?**
today	**dzisiaj**
tomorrow	**jutro**
yesterday	**wczoraj**
entrance	**wejście**
exit	**wyjście**
open	**otwarte**
closed	**zamknięte**
pharmacy	**apteka**
post office	**poczta**
theater	**teatr**
railway station	**dworzec kolejowy**
bus stop	**przystanek**
street	**ulica (ul.)**
square	**plac (Pl.)**
avenue	**Aleja (Al.)**
boulevard	**skwer**
market square	**Rynek**
city center	**centrum**
bridge	**most**
square	**plac**
cathedral	**katedra**
exchange office	**kantor**
town	**miasto**
ticket office	**kasa biletowa**
currency exchange	**kantor**
bill/check	**rachunek**
shop	**sklep**
town/city	**miasto**
castle	**zamek**
church	**kościół**

Poland

old town	**stare miasto**
old town square	**rynek**
town hall	**ratusz**

DAYS OF THE WEEK

Monday	**poniedziałek**
Tuesday	**wtorek**
Wednesday	**środa**
Thursday	**czwartek**
Friday	**piątek**
Saturday	**sobota**
Sunday	**niedziela**

NUMBERS

zero	**zero**
one	**jeden**
two	**dwa**
three	**trzy**
four	**cztery**
five	**pięć**
six	**sześć**
seven	**siedem**
eight	**osiem**
nine	**dziewięć**
ten	**dziesięć**
eleven	**jedenaście**
fifteen	**piętnaście**
sixteen	**szesnaście**
seventeen	**siedemnaście**
eighteen	**osiemnaście**
nineteen	**dziewiętnaście**
twenty	**dwadzieścia**
thirty	**trzydzieści**
forty	**czterdzieści**
one hundred	**sto**

M

MAPS

Tourism Information Offices routinely supply visitors with free maps of cities (and regions, often for a nominal fee) that are sufficient for most peoples' purposes. There are plenty of more comprehensive maps available, published by PPWK and others. Those driving through Poland may want to purchase a Road Atlas (Atlas Samochodowy).

MEDIA

Newspapers and Magazines. *The Warsaw Voice* is a weekly English-language newspaper with a business slant. Other papers to look for include Welcome to Warsaw (a free information sheet), *Warsaw Insider* (free quarterly with cultural listings), and *In Your Pocket* (Warsaw, Kraków, and Gdańsk editions—mini-guides with lots of listings and pertinent information). Western newspapers, including *The International Herald Tribune, Financial Times,* and *USA Today,* arrive the day of publication. Others may arrive a day or two late.

Radio and Television. Polish Radio 1, at varying frequencies across Poland, broadcasts headline news in English. There are two Polish state TV channels and PolSat, a private channel. All hotels with four or more stars (and some three-star hotels) offer satellite television with major European and American channels and news programs.

MONEY *(pieniądze)*

Currency. The unit of currency is the złoty (zł). Coins in circulation include 1, 2, and 5 zł. Banknotes come in denominations of 10, 20, 50, 100, and 200 zł. One złoty equals 100 groszy (gr), which you'll see in 1, 2, 5, 10, 20, and 50 coin denominations.

Currency Exchange. Foreign currency can be exchanged at the airports and banks, as well as most hotels. Kantors are ubiquitous private exchange houses, often very informal-looking, that exchange cash only. They offer the best rates (no commission). Your passport is only necessary when changing money at banks. It's wise to keep all your exchange receipts until you leave the country. The exchange rate at press time was slightly more than 4 zł to the US dollar. There is no black market for currency in Poland.

Credit cards. Major international credit cards (Visa, Mastercard, and American Express) are increasingly accepted in most hotels, restaurants, and shops, but are not accepted everywhere. In some cases, only one of the above credit cards will be accepted. You are usually unable to pay using a credit card at supermarkets, museums, and even train stations.

ATMs. Cash machines, known as "Bankomats," (PLUS and Cirrus networks and major credit cards) are widespread in Polish cities and offer competitive international exchange rates. They dispense cash in Polish zł.

Traveller's checks. These may be cashed at all of the above outlets except kantors and may sometimes be substituted for cash, but you'll almost certainly get a much poorer rate of exchange than if you convert them to cash. Commission is generally 1 to 2%.

ATM	**bankomat**
cash	**gotówka**
bank	**bank**

OPEN HOURS (See also PUBLIC HOLIDAYS)
Most businesses in Poland are open 8am–5pm Monday–Friday. Supermarkets, department stores, and shopping centers are open 9am-8pm, Monday-Saturday; Sunday, 10am-6pm. Smaller shops are open 10am-6pm Monday to Friday, 9 or 10am-11 or 12pm Saturday. Some close all day Saturday. For 24-hour shopping look for the sign "Non-Stop." Banks are generally open 9am–4pm Monday–Friday (some close at 1pm on Friday). Museums are usually closed on Monday. They are open 10am–6pm Tuesday–Sunday. Post offices

are open 8am–8pm Monday–Friday, 8am-2pm Saturday. The Central Post Office in Warsaw is open 24 hours (see POST OFFICE).

POLICE *(policja)* (See also CRIME AND Safety and EMERGENCIES)
Police emergency: Tel. 997
Warsaw Police Headquarters: ul. Wilcza 21.

    police station   **posterunek policji**

POST OFFICES *(poczta)*

Post offices handle mail, telephone, telegraph, telex, and (at the larger offices) fax. Stamps can also be purchased at tobacconists or in stores where postcards are sold. Red mailboxes on the street are marked "Poczta."

The Central Post Office (Poczta Główna) in Warsaw (ul. Świętokrzyska 31/33; Tel. 826 60 01) is open 24 hours. Other branches are Warszawa 120 (Centralna Train Station; Tel. 825 44 16; open Mon-Fri 8am–8pm, Sat 8am-2pm) and Warszawa 19 (Okęcie International Airport, Terminal 1; Tel. 846 06 86). There are perhaps a dozen more branches in Warsaw.

In Kraków, the Central Post Office is located at ul. Wielopole 2; Tel. 422 24 97; open 7:30am-8:30pm Mon-Fri, Sat 8am-4pm, Sun 9am-11am. A second branch is opposite the train station, at ul. Lubicz 4/Pl. Kolejowy; open 7am-8pm Mon-Fri.

International postcards and letters to Europe cost 1.90 zł; to the U.S. and Canada, 2.10 zł.

DHL, Federal Express, and UPS all have offices in Warsaw and Kraków.

    letter   **list**
    stamp   **znaczek**
    air mail   **poczta lotnicza**

Poland

PUBLIC TRANSPORTATION
Local Transport
Most Polish cities have well-developed systems of public transport that include buses and trams (and in the case of Warsaw, a single Metro, or subway, line).

In Warsaw, 1,200 buses operate from 5am to 11pm; night buses go from 11:30pm to 5:30am. Tickets (good for buses, trams and the Metro) can be purchased at kiosks with a green-and-yellow Ruch logo, and you can also buy a ticket directly from the driver for a slightly higher price. Validate your ticket upon boarding (old punchcards are being phased out in favor of magnetic-strip cards). Ticket inspectors issue fines on the spot for traveling without a validated ticket.

In Kraków, there are 22 tram lines and more than 100 bus lines. They run from 5am-11pm. You can purchase single-trip tickets, one-hour tickets, one-day and one-week passes.

For municipal transport assistance, call Tel. 9484.

Buses *(autobus)*. Most city buses tend to be red. Fast buses and night buses are twice as expensive as normal day buses. Signal that you want to get off by pressing the bell.

Trams *(tramwaj)*. Trams, or streetcars, cover large networks in most Polish cities; some run throughout the night. Departure schedules are posted, though they may not be strictly adhered to. In Warsaw, there's an Old Town street car that begins and ends its route at Castle Square, taking a 30-minute guided trip through the Old and New Towns (12 zł; Tel. 501 131 245.

Taxis *(taxi/taksówka)*. Taxi fares should start at 5 zł and go up 1.4 zł every additional kilometer (at night, 2 zł). Polish taxis are notorious for overcharging foreigners. So-called "mafia taxis" are ubiquitous, and very difficult for the uninitiated to tell apart from registered, legal cabs. The mafia taxis line up at airports and train stations with impunity. If you want a taxi, you should always call for one; ask your hotel to call a Radio Taxi (Tel. 919). Also, see taxi companies listed on page 148.

Hailing a cab is not recommended. Taxis hailed in the street will almost certainly be mafia cabs. If it's an emergency, agree upon the fare in advance.

Subway or Underground *(Metro)*. The recently opened Metro in Warsaw operates a single 13-km (8-mile) line that runs from the city center to the southern suburb of Kabaty (near Ursynów). It functions daily 4:30am-11:30pm, with trains every 5 minutes during rush hour, every 15 minutes during off-peak hours.

Transport around the country

Buses/Coaches *(autobus)*. Warsaw's main bus station is Warszawa Zachodnia (Warsaw West) (Al. Jerozolimskie 144; Tel. 9433). Kraków's main bus station is Dworzec (ul. Worcella; Tel. 9316). Gdańsk's bus station is Dworzec PKS (ul. 3 Maja 12; Tel. 302 00 48).

The national bus service, PKS (Polish State Bus Service), has the most extensive network of bus routes throughout the country. A private alternative is Polski Express (Tel. 22/620 03 30).

Bus information, domestic: Tel. 9433

Bus information, international: Tel. 22/823 57 70

Trains *(pociąg)*. Train is by far the most common and best way to travel between major cities, with the exception of short journeys for which buses are faster (Kraków-Zakopane, for example). Warsaw has six train stations; most international trains arrive at Warszawa Centralna (Al. Jerozolimskie 54; Tel. 9436), while others go to Warszawa Wschodnia. Smaller stations, mostly on the edges of the city, handle regional trajectories.

Kraków's main railway station is Kraków Dworzec Główny (Pl. Dworcowy 1; Tel. 624 54 39); it handles international and inter-city bus routes. Gdańsk's train station is Gdańsk Główny (ul. Podwale Grodzkie 1; Tel. 301 11 12); a commuter train travels among the three components of the Tri-city, leaving every 10 minutes between 6am-7:30pm and less frequently thereafter. The journey from Warsaw to Kraków takes 3 hours; Warsaw-Gdańsk, 3 hours 40 minutes; Warsaw-Poznań, 3 hours 20 minutes.

Poland

Tickets can be purchased at the train station in advance or on board from the conductor (for a surcharge).

Train timetables and information: Tel. 9436 or 9431 or www.pkp.com.pl.

ticket kiosk (buses/trams)	**sprzedaż biletów MPK**
ticket	**bileł**
reserved seat ticket	**miejscówka**
departure	**odjazdy**
arrival	**przyjazd**
Please, a ticket to…	**Proszę bilet do…**
return	**bilet powrotny**

R

RELIGION

Nearly all native Poles are Roman Catholic, and as many as 80% are practicing Catholics. Pope John Paul II was a Cardinal and Archbishop of Kraków before becoming the head of the Catholic Church. Mass is said in Polish. Other minority faiths, notably Protestant, Eastern Orthodox, and Jewish, are also represented.

Tourism Information Offices should have a list of services held in English and other languages (infrequent).

T

TELEPHONE (telefon)

Most public phones now are phone-card only—but that doesn't mean that all of them are in working order. Phone cards (25, 50 or 100 units—7.50 zł, 15 zł or 30 zł) may be purchased at newsstands, some hotels, post offices, and tourist information (IT) offices. Long distance and international calls can also be made in Warsaw at Netia

Telephone (ul. Poleczki 13; Tel. 648 45 00; open 8:30am–5pm Mon-Fri) and TPSA (ul. Nowy Świat 6/12; Tel. 627 40 81). In Kraków, Telepunkt (Rynek Główny 19; Tel. 429 17 11; open 8am-10pm Mon-Fri, weekends 10am-6pm; discounted phone cards) and Netia Telephone (ul. J. Conrada 51; Tel. 291 00 07).

To make an international call from a public phone, dial the international access code (0—listen for tone—0-tone), followed by the country code and telephone number, including area code. There are no off-peak rates for international calls. For long-distance national calls, dial the area code (preceded by zero) and number; off-peak rates start at 10pm. Local calls do not require the area code. Mobile telephone numbers have 10 digits.

Local directory assistance: Tel. 913.

Inter-city directory assistance: Tel. 912.

International directory assistance: Tel. 908

Area codes: Gdańsk/Gdynia/Sopot, (0)58; Kraków, 12; Poznań, 61; Toruń, 56; Warsaw, 22; Zamość, 84; Zakopane, 18

public telephone	**automat telefoniczny**
telephone card	**karta telefoniczna**

TIME ZONES

All of Poland is in the same time zone, Central European Time, or Greenwich Mean Time + 1 hour (or US Eastern Standard Time + 6 hours). Daylight savings time in summer (GMT + 2) is in effect from the last Sunday in March.

New York	London	Warsaw	Jo'burg	Sydney	Auckland
6am	11am	noon	noon	8pm	10pm

TIPPING

Tipping is the norm in Poland but not obligatory. It's customary to leave 10-15% at restaurants and round up the bill at bars. Some restaurants may add on a 10% tip; look carefully at the bill and ask if this appears to be the case to avoid tipping twice. Porters, maids, and tourist guides also expect tips.

TOILETS (*toaleta publiczna*)

In Poland all toilets are pay toilets. Even restaurants commonly charge patrons (1-2 zł) for use of their facilities. Men's rooms are commonly denoted by triangle symbols; women's rooms, by circles.

men's room	**męski (panowie)**
women's restroom	**damski (panie)**

TOURIST INFORMATION (*informacja turystyczna*)

Tourist information is dispersed among several entities.

Warsaw: Warszawa IT is located at Okęcie airport arrivals terminal; Centralna Railway Station (main hall, ul. Jerozolimskie 54); Historical Museum of Warsaw (Old Town Market Square, or Rynek Starego Miasta 28/42); and Western Bus Station (Al. Jerozolimskie 144). These are open daily from 8am-8pm. Another IT office is: Pl. Zamkowy 1/13; Tel. 635 18 81 (open 9am-6pm Mon-Fri, 10am-6pm Sat and 11am-6pm Sun). For general tourist information, call Tel. 9431.

Kraków: Kraków IT is found at ul. Szpitalna 25; Tel. 432 00 60; open 8am-4pm Mon-Fri. Centrum Informacji Turystycznej, a private office, is in the Cloth Hall (Rynek Główny 1/3; tel 428 36 00; open 9am-6pm Mon-Fri, Sat 9am-1pm).

Gdańsk: Centrum Informacji Turystycznej (ul. Hewelisusza 27; Tel. 301 43 55; open 9am-6pm Mon-Fri).

Poznań: Centrum Informacji Meijskiej (ul. Ratajczaka 44; Tel. 9431 or 851 96 45); Tourism Information Center, Stary Rynek 59 (Tel. 852 61 56).

Toruń: Wojewódzki Ośrodek Informacji Turystycznej (ul. Piekary 37; Tel. 621 09 31).

Zamość: Centrum Informacji Turystycznej (ul. Kościuszki 17; Tel. 201 22 11).

Zakopane: Zamojski Ośrodek Informacji Turystycznej (Town Hall, Rynek Wielki; Tel. 639 22 92).

Before you leave home, you can write, call or visit the Web site of the Polish National Tourism Office for general information:

U.K.: Polish National Tourist Office, First Floor, Remo House, 310-312 Regent Street, London W1R 5AJ; Tel. (0171) 580-88-11. http://w3.poland.net

U.S.: Polish National Tourist Office, 275 Madison Avenue, Suite 1711, New York, NY 10016; Tel. (212) 338-9412. <www.poland-tour.org>

W

WEB SITES

www.polandtour.org (Polish National Tourism Office)

www.hotelspoland.com (hotel clearing house)

www.warsawvoice.com.pl (site of English-language weekly)

www.Kraków.pl (municipal site)

www.warsawtour.pl (municipal site)

www.pkp.com.pl (Polish state railway schedules)

www.polishvodkas.com (self-explanatory)

WEIGHTS AND MEASURES

Weight

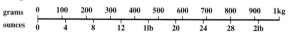

grams	0	100	200	300	400	500	600	700	800	900	1kg
ounces	0		4	8	12	1lb	20	24	28	2lb	

Poland

Temperature

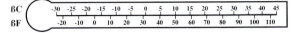

Fluid measures

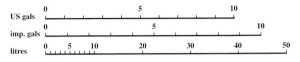

YOUTH HOSTELS *(schroniska młodzieżowe)*
There is an extensive network of youth hostels—reportedly as many as 950 in all—throughout Poland. For additional information, contact the Polish Association of Youth Hostels (ul. Chocimska 28, Warsaw; Tel. 22/498 12 28). International Student Hostels Accommodations are available through the ALMATUR Travel Bureau (ul. Kopernika 23, Warsaw; Tel. 22/826 35 12). Hostels in Warsaw include the extremely clean Agrykola (ul. Myśliwiecka 9; Tel. 622 91 10), and Student Hostel (ul. Żwirki i Wigury 97/99; Tel. 668 63 07); in Kraków, YHA Hostel (ul. Oleandry 4; Tel. 633 88 22), Dom Turysty PTTK Hostel (ul. Westerplatte 15; Tel. 12/422 95 00), and Student Hostel (ul. Bydoska 19; Tel. 12/423 79 32).

Recommended Hotels

Hotels in Poland are graded from one star to five stars, though the rating may weigh the age of the building equally against other factors like services and rooms. Poland's roster of quality visitor accommodations has improved but, especially at the mid- to lower-range, choices are limited. International chains and joint ventures have moved in to compete with the longtime hotels operated by big Polish chains like Orbis and Gromada. It is always wise to book ahead, particularly for June, July, August, and September.

The following guide denotes the rack rate price of a double room with bath/shower in high season (May through October, as well as Christmas) including breakfast and VAT. Hotel room rates are variously quoted in US dollars, euros, Polish złoty, and German marks (DM) — though the bill will ultimately be rendered in złoty. All accept major credit cards, except where noted.

Most local tourism information offices also have lists of private accommodations.

$	under $30
$$	$30-$70
$$$	$70-$120
$$$$	$120-$200
$$$$$	$200 +

KRAKÓW

Hotel Maltański $$$ *ul. Straszewskiego 14; Tel. 12/431 00 10, fax 12/431 06 15; <www.maltanski.pl>.* A new, modern, and elegant small hotel in a renovated 19th-century building on the southwestern edge of the Planty. Classy rooms, good service, and breakfast. Walking distance to Wawel Hill and all major sights. Wheelchair access. 30 rooms.

Poland

Hotel Copernicus $$$$$ *ul. Kanonicza 16; Tel. 12/431 10 44, fax 12/431 11 40; <www.hotel.com.pl>*. On one of Kraków's most atmospheric streets, this is the city's newest and grandest hotel. It is located in a marvelously restored 16th-century building just minutes from Wawel Hill. Rooms are very elegant, furnished with well-chosen antiques. Wheelchair access. 29 rooms.

Grand Hotel $$$$ *ul. Sławkowska 5/7; Tel. 12/421 72 55, fax 12/421 83 60; <www.grand.pl>*. A stylish 19th-century hotel with stained-glass-lined hallways and classic furnishings, the Grand is one of the best hotels in the heart of Old Town. Rooms were nicely renovated about a decade ago. Some suites are very posh. Elegant courtyard restaurant. Wheelchair access. 56 rooms.

Hotel Francuski $$$ *ul. Sławkowska 5/7; Tel. 12/422 51 22, fax 12/422 52 70; <www.orbis.pl>*. This handsome Orbis hotel, built in 1912, is on the edge of Old Town, facing the Planty near the old embattlements. Rooms are luxurious if a tad dated in style. Wheelchair access. 42 rooms.

Hotel Pollera $$$ *ul. Szpitalna 30; Tel. 12/422 10 44, fax 12/422 13 89; <www.pollera.com.pl>*. Art lovers will like this traditional 150-year-old hotel the moment they enter the lobby. A stained-glass window by Kraków artist Stanislaw Wyspiański hangs over the staircase. Rooms are old-fashioned but nicely equipped for the price. Close to the Opera House and Market Square. Wheelchair access. 42 rooms.

Hotel Eden $$$ *ul. Ciemna 15; Tel. 12/430 65 65, fax 12/430 67 67; <www.hoteleden.pl>*. A small and friendly new hotel leading a revival of the old Jewish quarter, Kazimierz. Simple and modern furnishings in a renovated 15th-century building. Good pub, Ye Old Goat, downstairs. Wheelchair access. 27 rooms.

Hotel Saski $$$ *ul. Sławkowska 3; Tel. 12/421 42 22, fax 12/421 48 30.* An enviably located old-style hotel smack in the middle of Old Town, on one of its nicest streets. Rooms are either very traditional and very frilly, or rather plainly modern. Wheelchair access. 56 rooms.

Hotel Sarp $$ *ul. Floriańska 3; Tel. 12/292 02 66, fax 429 17 78. <www.hotel-sarp.com.pl>.* A well-located tiny guesthouse, formerly part of the Polish Arquitect's Union. Nice details and hardwood floors, but mostly shared baths and a 4-flight walk-up. But it's on classic, but busy, Floriańska Street. Good budget option. 6 rooms.

Hotel Rezydent $$$ *ul. Grodzka 9; Tel. 12/429 54 95, fax 12/429 55 76; <www.rthotels.com.pl>.* A great location if you want to be in the thick of things: on the street with the most foot traffic leading off the Market Square. Appropriately ancient on the outside, fresh and modern on the inside. Triples and a huge apartment for four available. 50 rooms.

Pod Różą $$$$ *ul. Floriańska 14; Tel. 12/422 12 44, fax 12/421 75 13; <pod-roza@hotel.com.pl>.* One of Kraków's most elegant hotels is this mid-size charmer on famous Floriańska street. The 14th-century building has recently been totally renovated in grand style. Chandeliers and arched ceilings await guests. Wheelchair access. 50 rooms.

ZAKOPANE

Hotel Litwor $$$-$$$$ *ul. Kropówki 40; Tel./fax 18/201 71 90.* On a small side street off Zakopane's main shopping promenade, this large, handsome chalet is one of the chicest in town. It has an agreeable lobby bar, nicely furnished rooms, an indoor pool, and fitness center with sauna. Wheelchair access. 55 rooms.

Poland

Hotel Orbis Kasprowy $$$ *ul. Polana Szymoszkowa 1; Tel. 18/201 43 10; fax 18/201 52 72; www.orbis.pl.* This massive resort hotel, part of Poland's largest chain, lies about a mile west of town. It abounds in amenities: pool, sauna, gym, restaurant, satellite TV. Wheelchair access. 288 rooms.

Sośnica Lipowy Dwór $$$ *ul. Heleny Modrzejewskiej 7; Tel. 18/206 67 96, fax 18/201 43 36.* In a residential park of Zakopane, this large comfortable hotel is near to the main shopping promenade but pretty quiet. Rooms are serviceable. Wheelchair access. 38 rooms.

ZAMOŚĆ

Zamojski Hotel $$$ *ul. Kollataja 2/4/6; Tel. 84/639 25 16, fax 84/639 28 86; <www.orbis.pl>.* This hotel, occupying six nicely renovated 16th-century townhouses next to Town Hall on the magnificent Rynek, is one of the Orbis chain's best efforts. Stylishly modern, but respectful of the original architecture, the buildings are connected by lovely interior courtyards. Wheelchair access. 53 rooms.

Arkadia $$; *Rynek 9; Tel. 84/638 65 07.* An enviable location, right on one of Poland's finest Renaissance main squares, this tiny hotel is a worthy alternative to the more upscale Orbis hotel around the corner. 4 rooms.

WARSAW

Sheraton Warsaw $$$$$ *ul. Prusa 2; Tel. 22/657 61 00, fax 22/657 62 00; <www.sheraton.com/warsaw>.* The hotel of choice for international business travelers, the very modern and elegant Sheraton is well-located, about halfway between Łazienki Park and the Old Town. Rooms are luxuriously appointed, and "smart rooms" are completely outfitted with work facilities. Excellent gym, restaurants, services. Wheelchair access. 352 rooms.

MDM Hotel $$$$ *Pl. Konstytucji 1; Tel. 22/621 41 76, fax 22/621 41 73.* It would be hard to be more in the thick of things than at this large hotel on Constitution Square. The building is typical of 1950s Polish architecture, and the standard décor is a bit dated, but rooms are large and it's a fair deal for the location. Wheelchair access. 120 rooms.

Le Royal Méridien Bristol $$$$$ *ul. Krakowskie Przedmieście 42/44; Tel. 22/625 25 25, fax 22/625 25 77; <www.lemeridien-hotels.com>.* The most luxurious traditional hotel in Warsaw is this beautiful 1901 Beaux Arts building with elegant furnishings throughout. Grand but not pretentious, it's next door to the presidential palace and walking distance to Warsaw's swankiest shopping and Old Town. Rooms are gorgeous with classic styling. Fitness center, pool, sauna, well-equipped business center. Wheelchair access. Great café, restaurant. 206 rooms.

Hotel Europejski $$$-$$$$ *ul. Krakowskie Przedmieście 13; Tel. 22/826 50 51, fax 22/826 11 11; <www.orbis.pl>.* This Orbis hotel, across from the landmark Bristol, first opened in 1857. Rooms are somewhat more functional than the grand exterior would lead you to believe. Nonetheless, great location. Wheelchair access. 247 rooms.

Hotel Maria $$ *Al. Jana Pawła II NR 71; Tel. 22/838 40 62, fax 22/838 40 62.* A charming family-run hotel near the Powązki and Jewish cemeteries and within walking distance of Old Town. Friendly service, good restaurant, and nicely furnished modern rooms; an especially good option for those who don't like big corporate hotels. 22 rooms.

Holiday Inn $$$$$ *ul. Złota 48/54; Tel. 22/697 39 99, fax 22/697 38 99; <www.holidayinn.pl>.* Surprisingly luxurious edition of the American chain, with an excellent fitness center, room amenities, and business center. Not inexpensive, though, especially for a Holiday Inn. Wheelchair access. 346 rooms.

GDAŃSK

Hotel Hanza $$$$ *ul. Tokarska 6; Tel. 58/305 34 27, fax 58/305 33 86; <www.hanza-hotel.com.pl>.* Easily Gdańsk's best option in the Main Town. On the waterfront, this modern hotel is also just minutes' walk from the Long Market. Attractive and luxurious rooms with a clean aesthetic rather than fussy décor. Very good restaurant. Wheelchair access. 60 rooms.

Holiday Inn Gdańsk $$$ *ul. Podwale Grodzkie 9; Tel. 58/300 60 00, fax 58/300 60 03; <www.holidayinn.pl/ gdansk>.* This large American chain hotel is just across from the Gdańsk train station, and thus close to the highlights of Main Town, Old Town, and the now-quiet shipyards. Good service, quality business facilities, standard but well-equipped rooms. Wheelchair access. 143 rooms.

Jantar $$ *ul. Długi Targ 19; Tel. 58/301 27 16, fax 58/300 60 03; <www.trojmiasto.pl/jantar>.* A quirky little hotel with a splendid location: right on the Long Market, only paces from Town Hall, St. Mary's, and the waterfront. Rooms are very simple; some might find them dumpy. Curious restaurant-cum-nightclub downstairs. 44 rooms. No credit cards.

Dom Aktora $$ *ul. Straganiarska 55/56; Tel./fax 58/301 59 01.* This low-key pension in the heart of Main Town has a reputation as a boarding house for actors and theater folks. Rooms are utterly simple, but very clean. 9 rooms. No credit cards.

Hotel Grand $$$ *ul. Powstancóv Warszawy 12/14, Sopot; Tel. 58/551 00 41, fax 58/551 61 24; <www.orbis.pl>.* Appropriately named, this impressive red-roofed hotel, a 1927 Art Nouveau landmark, sits facing the Gdańsk Bay in the chic seaside resort of Sopot. The hotel is refined but not pretentious. A surprisingly good deal. Wheelchair access. 104 rooms.

Villa Hestia $$$$ *ul. Władysława IV 3/5, Sopot; Tel./fax 58/551 21 00; <www.villa.hestia.pl>.* This tiny guesthouse, a chateau in Sopot, is an elegant and romantic retreat. Nice personal touches throughout. Chic enough for the president of Poland, a sometime guest. 5 rooms.

TORUŃ

Hotel Petite Fleur $$ *ul. Piekary 25; Te.l 56/663 44 00*; A new, cozy little hotel in the heart of Toruń's Old Town, just two blocks from the Market Square. The hotel — more like an inn — occupies an elegant Renaissance burgher house and is expanding into the one next door to keep up with demand. Rooms are large and comfortable. Very good restaurant downstairs in cellar. 6 rooms.

Hotel Zajazd Staropolski $$ *ul. Żeglarska 10/14; Tel. 56/622 60 60, fax 56/622 53 84; <www.hotel.torun.pl>.* One of the best options in Old Town, between the Copernicus Museum and St. Mary's Church, on one of Toruń's most storied streets. Comfortable and friendly; well-equipped rooms spread across three handsome townhouses. Good restaurant. 36 rooms.

Hotel Pod Orłem $$ *ul. Mostowa 17; Tel. 56/622 60 60, fax 56/622 53 84; <www.hotel.torun.pl>.* Large for the tiny Old Town, this functional hotel near St. Mary's Church is a perfectly fine place to stay, though it doesn't aim much higher than that. Decent restaurant. Wheelchair access. 100 rooms.

POZNAŃ

Hotel Royal $$$ *ul. Św. Marcina 71; Tel. 61/858 23 00, fax 61/853 78 84; <royalhotel@poczta.onet.pl>.* Set back from the busy shopping street Św. Marcina in a quiet courtyard is this exceedingly handsome small hotel. Refurbished with superb modern taste after a fire gutted it in the late 1990s, it is now one of the most comfortable hotels in the city, within easy walking distance to Old Town. Friendly staff and large rooms. Wheelchair access. 27 rooms.

HP Park Hotel $$$ *ul. Majakowskiego 77; Tel. 61/879 40 81, fax 61/877 38 30; <www.hotel-park.com.pl>.* A well-equipped, modern hotel on the banks of Lake Malta south of Poznań's city center. Excellent, friendly service and top-notch restaurant with lake views. Perfect for trade-show attendees. Wheelchair access. 27 rooms.

Dom Turysty $$ *ul. Stary Rynek 91; Tel./fax 61/852 88 93;. <www.hotel-park.com.pl>.* The best location in the city: right on the beautiful and historic Old Town Square. The reconstructed 18th-century palace is simple, betraying its former status as a youth hostel, with multi-bed dorm rooms in addition to singles and doubles. 27 rooms.

KAZIMIERZ DOLNY

Hotel Łaźnia $$ *ul. Senatorska 21; Tel. 81/81 02 98.* A small and friendly hotel, centrally located with a pretty good restaurant. Much in demand in high season. 6 rooms.

Hotel Zajazd Piastowski $$ *ul. Słoneczna 31; tel. 81/881 03 46; fax 81/881 03 46.* A large and pleasant chalet-style hotel, a couple of miles beyond the town center. Swimming pool and bicycle rental, horseback riding. 64 rooms.

Recommended Restaurants

The dining scene in Poland's cities has improved dramatically in recent years, and diners now have a wider choice of cuisines and types of restaurants than ever. The emphasis remains on Polish cooking, and for most visitors, delving into the national diet in restaurants both fancy and informal will be at the top of their list.

Book ahead wherever possible at top-tier restaurants in Kraków and Warsaw. Many restaurants remain open throughout the afternoon, and most stay open late, until 11pm or 12am. All the restaurants below accept major credit cards except where noted. The following guidelines denote an average three-course meal for one, excluding wine and service:

$	less than 15 zł ($4)
$$	15-40 zł ($5-10)
$$$	40-80 zł ($10-20)
$$$$	over 80 zł ($20+)

KRAKÓW

Café Ariel $$$ *ul. Szeroka 18; Tel. 22/421 79 20.* Open daily for breakfast, lunch, and dinner. In the heart of Kazimierz, the Jewish quarter, is this charming long-time Jewish (but non-kosher) restaurant. Upstairs, it's decorated with lodge-like animal trophies, which take a back seat to the nightly (8pm) performances by a klezmer music trio. Great fun.

Café Camelot $$ *ul. Św. Tomasza 17; Tel. 22/421 01 23.* Open daily for breakfast, lunch, and dinner. Fashionable and funky café — a good place to sip tea, have a beer, or enjoy a light meal, including breakfast. Excellent fresh salads, soups, and sandwiches, plus great desserts. Decorated with cool Polish folk art.

Chłopskie Jadło $$$ *ul. Św. Agnieszki 1; Tel. 22/421 85 20.* Open daily for lunch and dinner. The name means "Peasant Kitchen," an apt description of this excellent, rustic Polish restaurant near Wawel Hill. Fun, colorful log cabin décor and classic, robust dishes like wild boar's ribs, eel, and herring, plus half-liter beers and folk music — like a restaurant deep in the Polish countryside. Breakfast and free cake on Sundays. Another location is in Old Town, at ul. Św. Jana 3.

Da Pietro $$$ *Rynek Główny 17; Tel. 22/422 32 79.* Open daily for lunch and dinner. Right on the Market Square, in a delightful cellar, this is a good place to get an Italian fix without breaking the bank. Large portions and a good list of pastas.

Gospoda CK Dezerterzy $$-$$$ *ul. Bracka 6; Tel. 22/422 79 31.* Open daily for lunch and dinner. A homey and charming restaurant popular with Poles and foreigners resident in Kraków. A good mix of Polish and Austrian fare and very fairly priced.

Kwarnia Grill $ *Stolarska 8-10; Tel. 22/422 19 08.* Open daily 11am-3am (Sat-Sun 12pm-3am). A self-service "milk bar" with good and cheap Polish standards (beet-root soup, pierogis, borscht), plus friendly service and an attractive outdoor seating area, one block from the Market Square. Good for lunch or late after-bar munchies. No alcohol. No credit cards.

Metropolitan $$$ *ul. Sławkowska 3; Tel. 22/421 98 03.* Open daily for breakfast, lunch, and dinner. A sleek, international, cosmopolitan place, with varnished wood, leather chairs, and separate dining rooms not unlike elegant railroad cars. Chic house drinks and creative international cuisine, such as sole with lime and chili.

Pod Aniołami $$$ *ul. Grodzka 35; Tel. 22/421 39 99.* Open daily for lunch and dinner. A cool and elegant medieval-looking cellar with stone walls, wood tables, and carpets on the walls. There's also a breezy interior courtyard for outdoor dining in summer. Specializes in grilled dishes, specifically meat of all stripes.

Wiśniowy Sad $$ *ul. Grodzka 33; Tel. 22/430 21 11.* Open Mon-Sat for lunch and dinner. This Russian café/restaurant, dressed up like a drawing room with silk scarves on the tables, floral paintings, and a piano, looks like a place where an exiled Czar might come for a taste of home. Great for caviar and vodka, a full meal, or the fabulous signature cherry crepes.

U Stasi $ *ul. Mikołajska 16; Tel. 22/421 50 84.* Open Mon-Fri for lunch only (until 5pm). A tiny joint down a passageway off a busy Old Town street, this Kraków classic lunch haunt is a favorite of actors, lawyers, and students — anyone who likes a good, inexpensive homecooked meal. Polish specialties. Communal tables. No alcohol. No credit cards.

ZAKOPANE

Barowo Zohylina $$-$$$ *ul. Piłsudskiego; Tel. 18/120 45.* Open daily for lunch and dinner. This excellent highlander restaurant would be "big fun," as my Polish friend likes to say, even if the food weren't terrific (which it is). The rustic décor — a wooden lodge with fur pelts and stuffed critters — is the perfect backdrop for dishes like sour cabbage soup and deer goulash. A regionally costumed band (the waiters, mostly) plays mountain music with great showmanship. No credit cards.

Karczma Obrochtówka $$-$$$ *ul. Kraszewskiego 10A; Tel. 18/206 39 87.* Open daily for lunch and dinner. One of Zakopane's best regional restaurants, where you'll get a dose of highlander culture in the traditional garb of the waiters, and rustic mountain cooking from the kitchen. Enjoy Górale dance and music.

ZAMOŚĆ

Ratuszowa $ *Rynek Wielki 13; tel. 84/715 57.* Open daily for lunch and dinner. This pretty basic restaurant-café is located in the Town Hall on Zamość's impressive Rynek, or Old Town Square, and is perfect for a beer, snack or simple Polish meal (such as ever-popular Polish sausages or soups) at very inexpensive prices.

Restauracja Padwa $$-$$$ *ul. Staszica 23 (Rynek); Tel. 84/386 256.* Open daily for lunch and dinner. A cellar restaurant off the main square, it's a bit like a dimly lit dungeon, with massive columns and arches and vaulted ceiling. Though it has a vaguely pre-glasnost feel to it, with its glizty "drink bar" at one end, you can't go wrong with Padwa's upstanding Polish fare, such as pierogis and soups.

WARSAW

Adler $$$ *ul. Mokotowska 69; Tel. 22/628 73 84.* Open daily for lunch and dinner. Near the Sheraton hotel, this cozy and extremely popular German joint revels in wiener schnitzel, sausages, and big German biers. Large portions and an occasionally noisy clientele (must be all that beer). Reservations are recommended.

Blikle Café $-$$ *ul Nowy Świat 33; Tel. 22/826 66 19.* Open daily for breakfast, lunch, and dinner. Warsaw's most famous café, which dates to the 1870s, is a terrific place for coffee and a pastry, but it's also ideal for a good selection of nationality-themed breakfasts, light lunches, sandwiches, and salads. Elegant and addictive.

Blue Cactus $$-$$$ *ul. Zajączkowska 11; Tel. 22/851 23 23.* Open daily for lunch and dinner. When Warsaw's ex-pats, many of whom are Americans, get an itch for tasty Tex-Mex (fajitas, enchiladas, etc.), they head to this colorful and cheery place opposite the new Hyatt hotel (near Łazienki Park). Very popular spot.

Dyspensa $$$ *ul. Mokotowska 39; Tel. 22/629 99 89.* Open daily for lunch and dinner. An absolutely terrific-looking place decked out to look like a welcoming country kitchen. Very popular and atmospheric at night, when locals and a good many ex-pats pack it to enjoy international dishes like duck a l'orange.

Fukier $$$$ *Rynek Starego Miasta 27; tel. 22/831 10 13.* Open daily for lunch and dinner. Probably Warsaw's most famous restaurant, this taste of Bohemian elegance on the Old Town Square is usually packed with diplomats and well-heeled Varsovians and ex-pats. In a charming, antique-stuffed historic house, the emphasis is on Polish fare, and though touristy, is still the one place to eat if you've only one night in Warsaw. The menu leans heavily on game.

Gessler Karczma $$$-$$$$ *Rynek Starego Miasta 21; Tel. 22/831 44 27.* Open daily for lunch and dinner. Another of the great-looking Polish restaurants on Old Town Square, this one is more rustic and slightly better value than the other high-end places. Set in several rooms in the cellars of a townhouse, decorated like a country inn, it serves traditional and hearty Polish fare, rarely straying from game and meat.

Malinowa $$$$ *ul. Krakowskie Przedmieście 42/44; Tel. 22/625 25 25.* Open daily for lunch and dinner. What you might expect from the opulent Bristol Hotel: a refined Old

World restaurant serving excellent Polish and French gourmet cuisine. One of the city's most luxurious and sophisticated dining rooms.

Pod Samsonem $$ *Freta 3/5; Tel. 22/831 17 88.* Open daily for lunch and dinner. Affordable and well-prepared Jewish and Polish cooking in an old townhouse on the main street in New Town, just beyond the walls of Old Town Square. The attractively simple and low-key restaurant is three connected rooms, with a long bar. One of the best deals in the city. Friendly and extremely efficient service.

Suparom Thai $$$ *ul. Marszałkowska 45; Tel. 22/621 32 34.* Open daily for lunch and dinner. Along a busy street in the city center, this is certainly the best Thai restaurant in Warsaw (a place one couldn't exactly say is known for such a thing). Great pad Thai and many other noodle-based dishes and soups in a friendly and attractive atmosphere. The entrance is a little confusing; at the same address upstairs is a Chinese restaurant.

U Dekerta $$$-$$$$ *Rynek Starego Miasta 38/42; Tel. 22/635 65 11.* Open daily for lunch and dinner. Refined but not pretentious, a beautiful restaurant that's less of a scene than Fukier just across the square. Vaulted ceilings, elegant porcelain, and efficient service complement the exquisite Polish offerings like pork loin with plum sauce and baked potatoes.

GDAŃSK

Karczma $-$$ *ul. Długa 18; Tel. 58/346 37 29.* Open daily for lunch and dinner. A cute little café on Gdańsk's most famous street. Ideal for quick and unpretentious meals of Polish food served on unique ceramic plates.

Restauracja Kubicki $$-$$$ *ul. Wartka 5; Tel. 58/301 00 50.* Open daily for lunch and dinner. A homey, old-style establishment on the waterfront that is Gdańsk's longest-running family restaurant — since 1918. It serves the house specialty, "Old Style Polish Knuckle," and more appetizing-sounding meat, fish, and poultry dishes in a place your grandparents might take you: deep red and gold wall coverings, dark wood, and landscape paintings in gold frames — old world charm.

Restauracja Pod Łososiem $$$$ *ul. Szeroka 52/54; Tel. 58/301 76 520.* Open daily for lunch and dinner. Acclaimed as Gdańsk's finest formal restaurant, "Under the Salmon" is a beautifully ornate establishment that used to be the distillery and tasting room of the locally produced Goldwasser vodka, which is infused with flecks of 23-carat gold. Posh and plush, with a sophisticated international menu, this is the place in Gdańsk for a special night out.

Retman $$$-$$$$ *ul. Stagiewna 1; Tel. 58/319 92 48.* Open daily noon-midnight. Occupying a historic burgher's house near the waterfront and Royal Way, this appealing upscale restaurant serves regional Polish specialties like red borscht with lamb dumplings, trout and pike perch. Major credit cards.

Towarzystwo Gastromiczne $$$ *ul. Korzenna 33/35; Tel. 58/305 29 64.* Open daily for lunch and dinner. In the cellars of the Old Town Hall is this very fashionable new restaurant, with low vaulted ceilings, colorful modern furnishings, and a good soundtrack — which adds up to one of Gdańsk's hippest eateries. The creative menu includes some Polish favorites like sour soup (cream-based and loaded with sausage) but mostly features French and international dishes.

TORUŃ

Petite Fleur $$$ *ul. Piekary 25; Tel. 56/663 44 02.* Open daily for lunch and dinner. Torun's most elegant restaurant is in the brick-walled cellar of a spiffy boutique hotel in Old Town. With heavy ceiling beams, romantic lighting, and excellent service, it's the perfect place for locals to celebrate a special occasion and visitors to enjoy American rib-eye and T-bone steaks, and chateaubriand for two. There are also French and Polish specialties.

Zajazd Staropolski $$ *ul. Żeglarska 10/14; Tel. 56/622 60 60, fax 56/622 53 84.* Open daily for lunch and dinner. This laid-back and enjoyable family-style hotel restaurant serves pretty good Polish fare under the vaulted wooden ceilings of a 14th-century Gothic townhouse.

POZNAŃ

Gospoda Młyńskie Koło $$$ *ul. Browarna 37; Tel. 61/878 99 36.* Open daily for lunch and dinner. In a handsome old water mill nestled in woods on the outskirts of town (5 minutes from the Market Square), this folksy restaurant serves Polish grilled specialties like boar and duck stuffed with apples. Great desserts and a magnificent fireplace.

Gospoda Pod Koziołkami $$$ *Stary Rynek 95; Tel. 61/851 78 68.* Open daily for lunch and dinner. Right on the Old Market Square, this comfortable and convenient restaurant has a simple self-service area upstairs, perfect for lunch, and an elegant dining room in the brick cellar. Polish standards.

Stara Ratuszowa $$$ *Stary Rynek 55; Tel. 61/851 53 18.* Open daily for lunch and dinner. Probably Poznań's most atmospheric eatery, this cellar restaurant on the Old Market Square has booths decorated with theater costumes, candlelight, and a fantastic cellar pub. Elegant but hearty and rustic-flavored Polish cooking with cheery service.

INDEX